The EDGE of DESPAIR

DERICK BINGHAM

The Edge Of Despair

First Published 1991

Copyright © Derick Bingham 1991

All Rights Reserved

Printed And Published By

AMBASSADOR PRODUCTIONS LTD.
Providence House,
16 Hillview Avenue,
Belfast, BT5 6JR,
U.K.

ISBN 0 907927 72 6

Dedication

This book is dedicated to Tom and Grace Clark who have shown me exceptional kindness and who have only deepened my love of Scotland and its hearty, resilient people.

OTHER AMBASSADOR PRODUCTS
BY DERICK BINGHAM

BOOKS

PROMISES TO KEEP   *A Daily Devotional Based On Proverbs* £4:99
MORE THAN A DREAM   *A Study Of The Life Of Joseph* £2:25
LORD OF OUR JOURNEY *Devotional Insights* £2:25
WAITING FOR GOD   *Daily Help For Those Who Can't See The*
                                   Wood For The Trees £4:95

MULTIPLE AUDIO CASSETTE AND VIDEO PACKAGE

THE RELUCTANT HERO - A Study Of The Life Of Moses

Born After Midnight
Lessons Learned From Failure
Burning Bridges or Bushes
Lord Here Am I, Send Aaron!
When They All Stand up Against You
Plagues That Preach
The Night Noboby Slept
Between The Devil And The Deep Red Sea
Is The Lord Testing You?
Giving Up A Good Thing For A Better
Reverence, The Forgotten Attitude
The Believer's Occupational Hazards
What Bad Temper Can Do
Do Shadows Frighten You?

AUDIO CASSETTES £3:00 EACH • VIDEO TAPES £9:99 EACH

AVAILABLE FROM CHRISTIAN BOOK STORES
OR DIRECT FROM THE PUBLISHERS (Add Postage)

Foreword

Many years ago, on my appointment to the Chair of Medical Genetics at the Queen's University of Belfast, I had to give an inaugural lecture. My title, based on the observation made by Eliphaz when attempting to console the patriarch Job in his suffering, was 'Born unto Trouble.'

'For affliction does not come from the dust, nor does trouble sprout from the ground, But man is born unto trouble, as the sparks fly upwards.' (Job 5:6-7)

Not only as far as illness and disease are concerned, but indeed in every aspect of daily living, man is born unto trouble. That trouble may come in many guises; it could be loneliness, fear, depression, guilt, despair, grief, unhappiness or loss of a loved one. Where do we turn for help in times like these? The Psalms has always been a source of comfort and encouragement. Who hasn't been comforted when afraid and alone by the quiet reminder of that, 'The Lord is my shepherd, I shall not want.' Who hasn't felt strangled by the grip of guilt only to find the soothing relief from 'Blessed is he whose transgression is forgiven, whose sin is covered; Blessed is the man to whom the Lord does not impute iniquity.'

This book based on twelve psalms provides encouragement for those feeling the pressures of daily living. The author, Derick Bingham, ministers the Word of God at Crescent Church, Belfast every Tuesday evening. This ministry brings him into contact with many hundreds of people facing the numerous problems, burdens and difficulties of life. He has been used great by God in Christian counselling and these studies reflect the depth of his wisdom and empathy for those in need. Let me urge you to spend a few hours in the following pages. It could alter your life. It is a joy and a privilege to commend this book. May the Lord use the pages that follow to help you. When you have finished the last page, I'm sure you will agree with the author, that 'our troubles are outnumbered in quantity and outvalued in quality by our blessings.'

Professor Norman C. Nevin.

Introduction

I have to confess that this book on the psalms is very personal. I have given my own hearts reaction to these 12 psalms dealing with some of the deepest problems in human life. My experience in writing these reactions was akin to J. B. Philips' experience when he was translating the Scriptures. Philips said it was like re-wiring a house with the mains still switched on!

Again and again my spirit lifted as I pondered what these psalms were saying to my heart. Again and again I wanted to cry "But what this psalm says is true! It's really true!" I knew it was all true but having just toured 3,000 miles across Eastern Europe preaching the Scriptures and writing this book through the Soviet Union's upheaval of August 1991, I found a delicious calm stealing into my soul which was proving to me in a new, fresh way how really contemporary these psalms are for our day. Nearly every day, while writing, someone was murdered here in Northern Ireland and on one afternoon terrorists organised 40 bomb scares alone in the city of Belfast where I live.

I can tell you this book was not written in cosy times, anymore than the experiences which gave rise to these psalms were cosy. To people on the edge of despair I humbly send this book. May the Lord use it to draw you right back off the edge and closer to himself. Selah.

Derick Bingham

1

When You Feel God Has Forgotten You

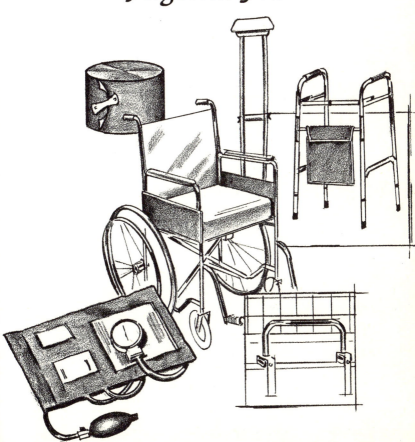

Psalm 73

Truly God is good to Israel,
To such as are pure in heart.

But as for me, my feet had almost stumbled;
My steps had nearly slipped.

For I was envious of the boastful,
When I saw the prosperity of the wicked.

For there are no pangs in their death,
But their strength is firm.

They are not in trouble as other men,
Nor are they plagued like other men.

Therefore pride serves as their necklace;
Violence covers them like a garment.

Their eyes bulge with abundance;
They have more than heart could wish.

They scoff and speak wickedly concerning oppression;
They speak loftily.

They set their mouth against the heavens.
And their tongue walks through the earth.

Therefore his people return here,
And waters of a full cup are drained by them.

And they say, "How does God know?
And is there knowledge in the Most High?"

Behold, these are the ungodly,
Who are always at ease;
They increase in riches.

Surely I have cleansed my heart in vain,
And washed my hands in innocence.

For all day long I have been plagued,
And chastened every morning.

If I had said, "I will speak thus",
Behold, I would have been untrue to the generation of your children.

When I thought how to understand this,
It was too painful for me ·

Until I went into the sanctuary of God;
Then I understood their end.

Surely you set them in slippery places;
You cast them down to destruction.

Oh, how they are brought to desolation, as in a moment!
They are utterly consumed with terrors.

As a dream when one awakes,
So, Lord, when you awake,
You shall despise their image.

Thus my heart was grieved,
And I was vexed in my mind.

I was so foolish and ignorant;
I was like a beast before you.

Nevertheless I am continually with you;
You hold me by my right hand.

You will guide me with your counsel,
And afterwards receive me to glory.

Whom have I in heaven but you?
And there is none upon earth that I desire besides you.

My flesh and my heart fail;
But God is the strength of my heart and my portion for ever.

For indeed, those who are far from you shall perish;
You have destroyed all those who desert you for prostitution

But it is good for me to draw near to God;
I have put my trust in the Lord God,
That I may declare all your works.

*R*ecently I stood in a graveyard in Romania. The door to a little stone building was open and I was led inside. Before me stood a stone table.

There, I was informed, people had been chained and tortured and acid was poured into the wounds inflicted on them. Their bodies were eventually carried to unmarked graves, nearby. After the revolution of 1989 some folk from a local church I was privileged to speak in happened to be going by the graveyard when they saw a crowd gather.

The crowd were digging up the bodies of their tortured friends. Photographs of the heart-breaking dig are displayed in one of the huge shop windows in the centre of Timisoara for the world to see. As I stood at that stone table the screams of those tortured victims seemed to cry out again. Deep inside me rose the questions that demand answers. Is there a silent Heaven? Had God forgotten these people? Could God forget anyone?

Evil, in whatever intellectual framework, is by definition a monster. Yet, the monster is charismatic. People find evil so much more attractive than good. Which films have the biggest attraction? The ones that romanticise evil. People like the doomed defiance of evil: there is a perverse fascination about it. Good is sweeter but it bores them.

Evil is so much easier than good. When Hitler was at Berchtesgaden, he loved to see the neighbourhood children and give them ice cream and cake. Saddam Hussein patted little Stuart Lockwood's head with chilling menace and asked if he were getting his cornflakes and milk. Stalin for years conducted the Soviet Unions business at rambling, sinister, alcoholic dinner parties that began at ten and ended at dawn. All his ministers attended, marinating in vodka and terror.

And they get off with it. A terrorist blasted a friend of mine to death on the very verge of his going out of Northern Ireland to be a christian missionary overseas. That good young life was murderously silenced while the terrorist rattles on with his political song and dance of horror. The oil fires over Kuwait are evil made visible but does Saddam Hussein repent? He laughs. The drug barons of South America are responsible for killing untold thousands but they live on in luxury. You may pay your taxes and refuse bribes and your business go under while plenty of others fiddle taxes and bribe their way to huge and lucrative contracts. You may have been more than faithful to your partner while he has been notoriously unfaithful to you. Your heart is broken while he enjoys every minute of his sin. The paradox is a problem for many people.

It certainly was to Asaph. There are twelve psalms in the Bible accredited to Asaph. He was a Levite of the Gershonite family and was appointed over the service of praise in the temple in the time of David and Solomon. He led the singing and sounded cymbals before the ark and, apparently set up a school of music. He was certainly a man of deep spiritual contemplative nature and he nearly came apart, spiritually, over the question of the prosperity of evil people and the apparent unrewarded life of the righteous. To him evil appeared the winner and good the loser. God seemed to have forgotten him.

Asaph states an accepted truism at the beginning of his psalm. "Truly God is good to Israel, to such as are pure in heart" (v.1). This is a quotation of what all good religions believe. They believed it in Israel. This is the theory. This is the axim of revealed truth. God is good to the upright. There was a huge overwhelming feeling that gripped Asaph, though, that caused his feet to nearly stumble and his steps to nearly slip. It was the feeling that stubborn facts contradicted the accepted wisdom. Was God really good to the righteous and opposed to those who traded in evil? The facts of experience seem to be at loggerheads with Scripture and Asaph lists the stark facts in no uncertain manner. He gives one of the most graphic portraits ever painted of what contemporary Americans would call a "Fat Cat". He even envies them.

For a start their bodies are healthy (v.4). They do not suffer like other people. They are free from the burdens that are common to humanity. "They are not in trouble as other men, nor are they plagued like other men"(v.5). Because they find they get away with it they wear pride like a woman wears a necklace. Pride, they reckon, looks good and they are certain it enhances them. They put on violence like you would put on your coat. Thomas Jefferson once wrote that "Barbarism has been receding before the steady step of amelioration: and will in time, I trust, disappear from the earth". His trust was ill placed. Violence in our world is everywhere. Even Bugs Bunny bashes, slams, blasts and shoots his way through children's television cartoon time to get laughs from millions of children. Elmer Fudd is the good guy! Violence is a very common coat from one end of the world to the other. Bad enough in cartoons but incredibly frightening in reality.

And evil people, do they suffer immediate wrath from God because of their violent lifestyle? Look at them, Asaph is saying, "Their eyes bulge with abundance, they have more than heart could wish" (v.7). They scoff, they defy Heaven and dictate to the earth. They are autocrats, people "fawn" on them. They mock saying that God doesn't even seem to know about them (v.11)! They seem immune to suffering, they are popular with the crowd and despite their breaking every law God has, they increase in wealth and are "always at ease".

"It just isn't fair", you can almost hear Asaph say. And his echo carries to our day. Look at the pornography kings, the thieves who escape detection, ramming Range Rovers through shop windows, look at the perpetrators of corruption, vice, violence, fraud and exploitation. The earth doesn't swallow them. No dread disease cuts them down. They flourish and their victims suffer. Is it really worth it to be a believer in such a world?

Asaph begins to examine where he stood and his immediate conclusion is that he has made a big mistake by trusting God and keeping his life clean. "Surely I have cleaned my heart in vain and washed my hands in innocence", he says (v,13).

Don't ever tell me that the Bible isn't realistic. Don't tell me that it is an ivory tower cut off from the real world where doubt and faith struggle day and night and evil and good are in deadly combat. It isn't. Asaph doubted God and his essential goodness and nearly got to the place where the Jews of the Holocaust got to in one concentration camp where they put God on trial with Rabbis as the judges. They found God guilty for not intervening on behalf of his people.

Asaph's dilemma is certainly a 20th Century dilemma. If there is an order in this Universe it seems desperately inaccessible. And Asaph didn't feel like talking to anyone about his doubt in case he betray his fellow believers. Is that how you feel? Are you lying in hospital writhing with pain while people who blaspheme God's name in every paragraph they speak, continue their lives, painless? Have you got to the place where you think God has other things on his mind rather than you? You feel he has forgotten you and you can't talk to anyone about it. Right? Then let Asaph talk to you.

One day Asaph walked into the temple. In those days God lived in the temple and his people were called to approach him. God loved his people and his great desire was to be with them and to have them before him. Asaph, it seems, went one day to the temple to pray and as he prayed his perspective suddenly changed and he saw his dilemma in an entirely new light. He suddenly realised that he had been concentrating on the present prosperity of evil men and women. His time scale was all wrong. As he stood before God he looked past their present success to their final destiny. It brought him up with a jolt and he saw very clearly the false basis of his thinking which had made him feel God had forgotten him.

"Surely you set them in slippery places: you cast them down to destruction. Oh, how they are brought to desolation, as in a moment! They are utterly consumed with terrors. As a dream when one awakes, so, Lord, when you awake, you shall despise their image" (v.18-20). Asaph's feet might have slipped on the Rock of ages but they would never slip off it. The ungodly were on the slippery slope and would fall, in a moment, to irretrievable ruin. He was only a heartbeat away from an unending Heaven and they were only a heart-beat away from an unending Hell. It is true they got off with their evil for a time but the day of Judgment will find them defenseless and banish them to eternal perdition. To envy them was plain stupid. They lived in the narrow confines of time, the believer lives in the wide open spaces of eternity.

Perspective in the believers life is vital. God does not promise to judge the evildoers of this world immediately. If God cut the head off every one who broke his law we would all be headless. Christ Jesus came into the world to save sinners. If sinners repent and trust Christ as Saviour there is salvation for them but if they refuse his mercy they will most certainly receive his judgment. The triumph of the ungodly will be very short lived.

Asaph begins to see his own personal bitterness for what it really was. "I was so foolish and ignorant before you", he said (v.22). What crass stupidity to envy the wicked! What have they got in comparison to what the believer has? They are more concerned with making a living than making a life. Asaph now gives vent to a surge of faith. You will not find anywhere in the Old Testament a more sublime expression of personal faith.

Asaph describes his life as a believer as a journey with God. God is travelling with him and is waiting for him at the end of the road. God holds his hand and guides his footsteps. To know and enjoy God is deeply satisfying. Everything else eventually decays and fails, even the body and mind but, says Asaph, "God is the strength of my heart and my portion forever" (v.26).

So, as the psalm faces a constant question it also presents a very clear choice of alternatives. The wicked are described as "Far from God". They will perish. Their definition of "The good life" is a life of material prosperity and success. The alternative is real friendship with God because eternal life is to know God and his son Jesus Christ. The real "good life" is to be near God. Everything that evil ever had is as nothing in comparison with fellowship with God. Is there any greater question asked in the Bible than Asaph's "Whom have I in heaven but you?" His affirmation of faith that had climbed out of the pit of doubt could not be clearer; "there is none upon earth that I desire besides you". To know God is the supreme good.

Let me finish this study of psalm 73 with a story. It is not often virtually an entire congregation breaks down and weeps but it happened in my experience one afternoon in the city of Arrad in Romania. I was preaching on the subject of the intervention of God. I spoke of how God had intervened at the Flood and the Red Sea, through the prophets and at Calvary. Then I told my congregation of a visit I had made to Bucharest a few days previously.

In Bucharest I had viewed the misnamed Palace of the People, Ceausescu's monstrosity with its 7,000 rooms. Along the esplanade leading to the palace were the apartments built for the party faithful. I entered one of them and the faithful were there all right. Only they weren't the Communist faithful. They were christians who were manning Bucharest's first christian bookshop in 45 years.

An older man was printing christian literature in a large room at the back of the apartment and he told me the printing press came from the former East German Communist propaganda headquarters! What a turn around! What do you put it down to?, I asked. "The finger of God", he replied. "There is a verse is there not", he said with a smile "about He who sits in the Heavens, laughing?" Indeed there is. My congregation wept. I had to stop preaching. There were tears of joy everywhere. The Spirit of God had touched our hearts at a very deep level. The theology of Asaph was at work. Let it work in your heart too.

2

When You Are Depressed

Psalm 42

As the deer pants for the water brooks,
So pants my soul for you, O God.

My soul thirsts for God, for the living God.
When shall I come and appear before God?

My tears have been my food day and night,
While they continually say to me,
"Where is your God?"

When I remember these things,
I pour out my soul within me.
For I used to go with the multitude;
I went with them to the house of God,
With the voice of joy and praise,
With a multitude that kept a pilgrim feast.

Why are you cast down, O my soul?
And why are you disquieted within me?
Hope in God, for I shall yet praise him
For the help of his countenance.

O my God, my soul is cast down within me;
Therefore I will remember you from the land of the Jordan,
And from the heights of Hermon,
From the Hill Mizar.

Deep calls unto deep at the noise of your waterfalls;
All your waves and billows have gone over me.

The Lord will command his loving-kindness in the daytime,
And in the night his song shall be with me
A prayer to the God of my life.

I will say to God my Rock,
"Why have you forgotten me?
Why do I go mourning because of the oppression of the enemy?"

As with a breaking of my bones,
My enemies reproach me,
While they say to me all day long.
"Where is your God?"

Why are you cast down, O my soul?
And why are you disquieted within me?
Hope in God;
For I shall yet praise him.
The help of my countenance and my God.

Psalm 43

Vindicate me, O God,
And plead my cause against an ungodly nation;
Oh, deliver me from the deceitful and unjust man!

For you are the God of my strength;
Why do you cast me off?
Why do I go mourning because of the oppression of the enemy?

Oh, send out your light and your truth!
Let them lead me;
Let them bring me to your holy hill
And to your tabernacle.

Then I will go to the altar of God,
To God my exceeding joy;
And on the harp I will praise you,
O God, my God.

Why are you cast down, O my soul?
And why are you disquieted within me?
Hope in God;
For I shall yet praise him,
The help of my countenance and my God.

*S*evere depression is one of the major concerns of this century and it affects somewhere between one and two million people in the world. In terms of lost production it costs the world fifty billion pounds every year. One in every seven people and three times as many women as men will at some time in their lives experience what depression brings.

What does depression bring? It brings feelings of inadequacy, failure, worthlessness, and guilt to plague the mind. It seems as if everybody is watching you and being critical of every move and action you make. Trivial fears and anxieties become greatly exaggerated. Life has no purpose. Even sleep patterns are interrupted so that waking at two or three in the morning is not unusual. The word "depression" can be used to cover a whole range of feelings from a fleeting feeling of unhappiness to profound, enduring, suicidal hopelessness.

Depression is often disguised and may appear in the form of marriage conflicts, sexual problems, drug or alcohol dependence, aggression and violence and so called "personality problems". The problem strikes right across the human spectrum. Marilyn Monroe, Sylvia Plath, Elvis Presley, Vincent van Gogh, Janice Joplin, Dylan Thomas, F. Scott Fitzgerald, Judy Garland, are amongst the seemingly endless names of people who have suffered from severe depression. One adult in 250 attempt suicide and 10,000 succeed, every year. In fact the truth remains that most people lead lives of quiet desperation but sometimes the hiding in quietness is shattered when they can no longer cope and depression overwhelms them.

Of course christians suffer from depression just as much as anyone else. The problem for christians is that when depression hits they begin to feel that the Bible is irrelevant, prayer is pointless, forgiveness is impossible and God seems far away. They even begin to wonder if he exists at all! One of the most famous hymn writers of all time, William Cowper ("God moves in mysterious ways, his wonders to perform" etc.), was a manic depressive and tried to kill himself several times and wrote "Why is the scenery like this, I had almost said, why is every scene, which many years since I could not contemplate without rapture, now become at the best, an insipid wilderness to me?" Millions of believers like Cowper have known black despair.

The psalmist of Psalm 42-43 is suffering from severe spiritual depression. "Why are you cast down, O my soul?", he asks, "Why are you disquieted within me?" (v.5). He loves his Lord, that is unquestioned, in fact he thirsts for him "As the deer pants for the water brooks" but his thirst for God is being severely aggravated and this has brought on a real bout of depression. What has happened?

Every year an Israelite was required to visit Jerusalem three times to meet with God. Each time was for a major festival and evidently the psalmist's plans to meet with God and his people had been thwarted. Notice that the psalm is entitled "A Maskil", which means "an instruction, of the Sons of Korah". It has been suggested that the psalmist may have been one of the Korahites who were gatekeepers, watchers and musicians in the temple. He was a singer (v.11) and a harpist (43:4) but, for some reason or other he couldn't get to the temple because he was held up in Northern Palestine (v.6). He wistfully remembers the great days when he "Used to go with the multitude" to the house of God with the voice of joy and praise. The very sound of the thunder of waterfalls and mountain rivers in spate only led him to think more about his own troubles and the fact that he seemed to be drowning in them (v.7).

Frustrated plans are often a cause of deep depression. You thought God would allow you to do something which was perfectly legitimate, which his Word certainly did not condemn and for which your very heart cried out but circumstances beyond your control have you in a narrow corner from which there is, for the moment, no escape and from which there is no relief.

Take, for example, Charlotte Elliot who wrote the hymn "Just as I am". Have you any idea how that soul stirring hymn which has led to the conversion to Christ of multitudes came to be written? It came out of a circumstance not far removed from the psalmists. Miss Elliot, at 45 years of age was suffering from ill health. Her brother, an Anglican clergyman was planning the erection of St. Mary's Hall at Brighton as a school for the daughters of clergymen and it was decided to hold a bazaar in aid of the fund.

Miss Elliot's home was frantically busy with preparations for the bazaar but she could do nothing, actively, to help. She lay awake the night before the event gripped, like the psalmist, with a deep depression and overwhelmed with a feeling of utter uselessness in the active service of God. The depression got so deep that she began to question the reality of her whole spiritual life.

The next day, the day of the bazaar, when all the rest of the family were gone, leaving Charlotte lying on the sofa in great weakness, the doubts and fears and spiritual depression returned with fresh force and she felt she must fight out this battle once for all. Getting pen and paper she began to examine the truths which were the foundation of her faith. She thought of God's love for her, of Christ's death at Calvary on her behalf, of the promises of God in the Bible. A poem emerged which contained these wonderful words

Just as I am, though tossed about
With many a conflict, many a doubt,
Fightings within and fears without,
O Lamb of God, I come.

Charlotte's sister-in-law came in after some time to tell her of the progress of the bazaar and after reading the poem asked, for a copy. So it stole out from that quiet room of suffering to touch millions. It even arrived at the deathbed of William Wordsworth's daughter Dora and led to her conversion. Last time I was in Grasmere churchyard I stood and looked again at Dora's grave and mused on the engraving on her gravestone which is of a lamb and a cross and underneath it the words "Him that cometh to me I will in no wise cast out". The hymn had transformed her life and preaches a sermon to the tens of thousands of people who visit that famous graveyard. When I wrote to Dr. Billy Graham about what he thought of the hymn, because he has used it more than any living man, his great choirs singing it across the stadiums of the world, he kindly wrote back and said "I have told to many audiences the story of Charlotte Elliot and the circumstances under which she wrote 'Just as I am'. It is always a blessing and an inspiration. We have used 'Just as I am' almost exclusively in our Crusades since the beginning, unless we choose not to use any song at the invitation but we can document in our memory and in our files many instances of people who have said that the hymn was the deciding factor for them in coming to Christ".

Are your plans thwarted, like the psalmists? Is this giving you a sense of estrangement from God? Why not realise that God is in the thwarting? Why not realise that our disappointments can be his appointments leading to a far greater thing for us in the future? Most of the time I have been writing this chapter a helicopter has been buzzing above my house on surveillance duty in this city of trouble where I live. Quite frankly it drives me scatty! People get shot almost every day in this Province of tragic beauty where I am called at this time to work for God. I can think of more peaceful places to serve the Lord but this is his will for me at this time and I cannot describe to you the joy he gives me here in his service and the blessing he has poured out on my undeserving head. Our plans are so limited in comparison to his. His plans are best. For you, for me.

The second cause of depression for the psalmist is the scoffing of the heathen who keep asking him "Where is your God?" (42:3,10). The heathen had their visible gods that they could set up in their temples or homes. Here was the psalmist far from Jerusalem and claiming that the living God was invisible. The heathen mocked the psalmist by implying that his God certainly seemed to be as inactive as he was invisible. They implied that he certainly did not seem to vindicate His people when they were oppressed by their enemies. The psalmist gets so sensitive to their ridicule that he feels the sharp pain of their scoffing is like a mortal wound in his body (42:10).

Do you ever feel like that? Are you weighed down by thwarted plans and mocking scoffers until you are inwardly disturbed like the raging of the sea? Then, like Charlotte Elliot and like the psalmist you must have a talk with yourself. You, like them must refuse to give in to these moods of spiritual depression. As Warren Weirsbe has said, there are three answers to spiritual depression. We must, first, stop looking at ourselves and start looking at God. The psalmist uses "I" 14 times, "me" 16 times and "my" 21 times!. Second, we must stop looking at the past and start looking at the future. Third, we must stop searching for reasons and start resting on promises. I have found a lot of help from those helpful points. So, let's stop looking in and back and around but let's look up! "Why are you cast down, O my soul? And why are you disquieted within me? Hope in God: for I will yet praise Him, the help of my countenance and my God" (43:5).

I am well aware that for certain conditions of depression a patient may need medical help. In fact I have advised medical help for people I have counselled who were in very real need of it and who thankfully took it and greatly benefited by it. I have counselled many people over the years who have come to me as a Christian Bible teacher for help and I have noticed that where there is loss of appetite, constant fatigue, loss of interest, difficulties in concentration, general slowing up or excessive over activity and agitation, and thoughts of suicide, then the one seeking help is experiencing warning signs of a very real slide into illness and needs professional help.

I thoroughly recommend Dr. Richard Winter's book "The roots of sorrow" to all who suffer from depression or who have to counsel those who do. Dr. Winter was senior registrar in psychiatry at Bristol General Hospital. The book is published by Marshall's, now under the Collins label. In his book he says that the symptoms I have already listed are "A strong indicator that the depression has become so extreme that it needs to be treated more as an illness than a problem needing only counselling or psychotherapy". We ignore such signals at our peril.

On the other hand spiritual depression coming from thwarted plans and ridicule from unbelievers can be cured immediately by using the very method the psalmist used. Even your seeming disadvantage of circumstances can become in God's hands your greatest advantage. If you could ever get above your seeming disadvantage long enough to see how God could use you to impact the lives of others who are victims of circumstances, it would greatly encourage you. You can be mightily used by God if you refuse to let your seeming disadvantage turn you into a miserably depressed christian. Come on, think about the impact your distinctive message can have upon the world around you. Get out there and write a psalm-in-action for others to read, a psalm of praise and encouragement. You will lift others who are lost in the gloom of the personal swamp of depression. Go for it, ignore the scoffers and realise that the difficult place God has put you into is to your ultimate advantage. After all, if such a thing hadn't happened to the psalmist we wouldn't have had the psalm, would we?

3

When You Lose A Sense Of Wonder

Psalm 139

O Lord, you have searched me and known me.

You know my sitting down and my rising up;
You understand my thought afar off.

You comprehend my path and my lying down,
And are acquainted with all my ways.

For there is not a word on my tongue,
But behold, O Lord, you know it altogether.

You have hedged me behind and before,
And laid your hand upon me.

Such knowledge is too wonderful for me;
It is high, I cannot attain it.

Where can I go from your Spirit?
Or whence can I flee from your presence?

If I ascend into heaven, you are there;
If I make my bed in hell, behold, you are there.

If I take the wings of the morning,
And dwell in the uttermost parts of the sea,

Even there your hand shall lead me,
And your right hand shall hold me.

If I say, "Surely the darkness shall fall on me".
Even the night shall be light about me;

Indeed, the darkness shall not hide from you,
But the night shines as the day;
The darkness and the light are both alike to you.

For you have formed my inward parts;
You have covered me in my mother's womb.

I will praise you, for I am fearfully and wonderfully made;
Marvellous are your works,
And that my soul knows very well.

My frame was not hidden from you,
When I was made in secret,
And skilfully wrought in the lowest parts of the earth.

Your eyes saw my substance, being yet unformed.
And in your book they all were written,
The days fashioned for me,
When as yet there were none of them.

How precious also are your thoughts to me, O God!
How great is the sum of them!

If I should count them, they would be more in number than the sand;
When I awake, I am still with you.

Oh, that you would slay the wicked, O God!
Depart from me, therefore, you bloodthirsty men.

For they speak against you wickedly;
Your enemies take your name in vain.

Do I not hate them, O Lord, who hate you?
And do I not loathe those who rise up against you?

I hate them with perfect hatred;
I count them my enemies.

Search me, O God, and know my heart;
Try me, and know my anxieties.

And see if there is any wicked way in me,
And lead me in the way everlasting.

*S*ometimes when you look into someone's eyes you wonder if there is anyone at home. The hassle of life has got to them. They seem immune to joy. A little baby's eyes are so different. Everything is a discovery. Everything is new and fresh and interesting. To see adults and even teenagers who have lost a sense of wonder is a tragedy.

David was one of those special people who kept a sense of wonder through his life. He wrote about it, and, Psalm 139 captures his fascination with life, its origins and his Creator, perfectly. Here was no "So, what's new?", attitude. Here was sheer exultation in living and sheer excitement at knowing and walking with God.

The first thing that grips David is the wonder of God's knowledge of him as an individual (v.1-4). If the Queen walked up to you somewhere and said "Hello Mary, how are things at No. 12 Railway Cuttings", you would never get over it. How did she know your name? How did she know where you lived? The message of this psalm is that God not only knows your address, he knows every time you sit down and every time you stand up and every time you lie down. There is not a word you speak but the Lord knows it altogether. He knows not only what you said but why you said it, what you intended it to mean and even what it possibly tried to cover up.

Are you someone who has lost the sense of God's love for you? Goodness knows there are plenty of people who almost want you to apologise for breathing. That is not God's attitude to you. David uses a most memorable expression when describing God's relationship with him: "You have hedged me behind and before" (v.5). Imagine a life enclosed by God. That surely is significance, personified. How can you say you don't matter if God goes before and behind you? Is that not enough to deal with any hassle? As for David he says "Such knowledge is too wonderful for me: it is high. I cannot attain it" (v.6). It doesn't stop him enjoying it, though, does it?

The next thing that grips David is a sense of the wonder of God's presence, everywhere. "If I ascend into Heaven, you are there; if I make my bed in Hell, behold you are there" (v.8). If he meets the dawn, travels from East to West, walks in darkness or the noonday sun, God is everywhere. That fact may frighten an unbeliever but it needn't for, "God so loved the world that he gave His only begotten Son that whoever believes in Him should not perish but have everlasting life". That God is everywhere is one of the greatest comforts any human being can know.

Quietly, in the psalm, David turns to one of the most sensitive and miraculous subjects known to human life: the baby in the womb. If anything evokes a sense of wonder it is the unborn child. David shows very clearly that the unborn child has a very definite relationship with God. God is likened to a weaver skillfully forming a precious life. Notice the fact that David refers to himself in his pre-natal existence as "I". He says "My frame was not hidden from you when I was made in secret" (v.15). The medical word is "Biological continuum". The baby in the womb is a human being and its formation is simply staggering. Few would argue that it is one of the greatest of all wonders. Let's examine it.

In the 266 days from conception to birth the single fertilised egg becomes a staggeringly complex organisation of 200 million cells having increased the original weight one billion fold. Let's begin at 3-4 weeks. The embryo is so tiny, about 1/10th of an inch long. The mother may not even be aware that she is pregnant. Yet, the nervous system is established. The heart and blood vessels are established. The tiny buds of the arms are forming. The heart at this stage, in proportion to its body, is nine times as large as an adults. It has to be powerful to force the blood around the embryo but also around the umbilical cord.

As the second month of the baby's life begins, the dark circle of the eyes appears. The ear and the teeth begin development. Fingers are growing fast, though webbed at this stage. Though the embryo weighs 1/30th of an ounce it has all the internal organs of the adult at various stages of development, even buds for 20 milk teeth!

At 8-12 weeks the sex of the child becomes identifiable by microscope. The baby gets its oxygen in the blood brought in by the umbilical cord, not from the air. The body wall has grown from the spine forward and is joined at the front like a coat being buttoned. It's living quarters get cramped and as it gains in strength the mother gets kicked by the thrust of foot, knee and elbow. At 18 weeks its ear stands out from its head.

"I will praise you, for I am fearfully and wonderfully made", says David to God (v.14). Did you know that even nails are a special development? Toenails do not develop at the same time as fingernails. Sometimes one of the first things an attending nurse has to do after a baby is born is to clip its fingernails! At 28-30 weeks the baby's eyes are open and it has a good head of hair.

"Marvellous are your works, and that my soul knows very well", says the psalmist (v.14). One of those marvellous works is the creation of the umbilical cord which may even pass around the baby's neck and yet it does not choke. Why? Because the cord remains stiff and tends to straighten automatically when bent. It stays this way because the blood rushes through it at the speed of about 4 m.p.h.

At 34 weeks the fingernails reach the fingertips. At 38 weeks the toenails reach the toetips. Then they begin to extend beyond the fingernails and toetips. Your very fingernail is a special creation. Imagine what life would be like without your fingernail! God cares about you enough to give you ten! It proves he is not just into local church services, he is into fingernails in a big way. He made every one of them!

Then comes that incredible moment when by a 100 lb propulsive force the baby moves out from a world of warmth at 98 degrees F into room temperature, 20 degrees lower. Its eyes open so long to nothing but darkness are suddenly assailed by light. For the first time it must start getting oxygen from the air, so its first breaths must be strong enough to inflate all the tiny air sacs in its lungs. A good loud cry helps this by forcing the breath through faster and the baby's life in the outside world has begun.

Of course there may be a reader scanning these lines and you are not filled with wonder at the birth of your baby because it was born badly deformed. While others glow in the wonder of a new life, your heart is broken. Why does sickness, illness, deformity, and death come? They entered the world at the fall of man and have been with us ever since. The fact that Christ died on the cross for sin hasn't stopped the weeds growing in my garden, or deformity marring a lovely, precious new life. But will it, eventually?

In the temple of the Old Testament no deformed person was allowed to serve as a priest. Was that because God was against deformed people? Certainly not. It was because the service of the temple was an analogy of the coming new earth. The redemption wrought by Calvary's work will bring about the redemption of the very earth on which we live, and the transformation of our very bodies. You cannot redeem something which has not something of the original in it and the Bible teaches that our very bodies will be redeemed, despite aches and pains or cancers or blindness and deformity. The fall's work will be eliminated. Meanwhile, even though an apostle like Paul might not be allowed by God to have his own physical illness removed (Called by Paul a "Thorn in the flesh"), during his lifetime, he is promised that God's grace to deal with the problem will be sufficient for him (2. Cor 12:9). That grace, hurting one, will be sufficient for you, too.

David notes that God has written in his book the actual days of his life and the details of "His Substance" long before he was formed in the womb. So it is with you and me. Whether we would be left handed or right handed, good at the Arts or Sciences, blue-eyed or brown-eyed, all was known to our Creator. So, don't let anybody tell you that there is such a thing as an ordinary person. Everyone, including you, is special. David didn't spend his time moaning that he wished he was taller, or smaller or more this or that, he accepted the way he was made and gave thanks for it. In acceptance lay peace.

Another wonder overwhelmed David, and if anything it is probably the most surprising thing for any human being to realise. It is the wonder of God's thought life about us. "How precious also are your thoughts to me, O God! How great is the sum of them! If I could count them they would be more in number than the sand" (v.17-18). Have you ever taken a handful of sand in your hand? Try counting the grains and see how many there are. Any average beach would strain the mind of even an Einstein. God's thoughts about you are innumerable. Even when you are asleep he is thinking about you and when you awake, he is still there. When the hassle of life makes you forget God, he will never forget you. The last part of Psalm 139 is the hardest part to understand. David calls upon God to slay the wicked whom he says he hates with a perfect hatred. The last five verses of Psalm 139 seem completely out of sync with the rest of his beautiful writing on the wonders of God and his attributes. Would the God who creates lovely babies, slay the wicked?

The answer is that God will certainly judge the wicked and banish them to Hell. David is saying that God's enemies are his but because he hates their sin does not mean that he is incapable of kindness towards them. He is calling on God to do the judging. It is an imprecatory psalm. Sometimes, of course, God used the armies of Israel to bring about such judgments but only at God's instigation.

When Peter tried to kill in defence of his Lord he was immediately told to put his sword away. The theocracy of Israel is over. Christ's kingdom is not of this world, else would his servants fight. That's why Peter and company ran away from Christ in the Garden, not because they were afraid of the Romans, for Peter's sword weilding had certainly proved that, but because they were tired of Christ's insistence that his kingdom was going to be built, not by insurrection of Governments but by the power of his Gospel, alone.

When God gets angry it is not like our anger. It is completely rational, completely just. His judgments are also a source of wonder. They are part of his intrinsic greatness. If he did not judge he would not be God. And David knew that God would judge him too and calls on God to search him and try his heart and mind, to root out any wicked way in him and to lead him in the way everlasting.

Stop, in the nitty-gritty of life, today and regain your sense of wonder. It will lift tiredness and weariness and bitterness out of your day. It will cause you to bow your head and worship.

4

When You Are Looking For Answers

Psalm 19

The heavens declare the glory of God;
And the firmament shows his handiwork.

Day unto day utters speech,
And night unto night reveals knowledge.

There is no speech nor language
Where their voice is not heard.

Their line has gone out through all the earth.
And their words to the end of the world.
In them he has set a tabernacle for the sun.

Which is like a bridegroom coming out of his chamber,
And rejoices like a strong man to run its race.

Its rising is from one end of heaven,
And its circuit to the other end;
And there is nothing hidden from its heat.

The law of the Lord is perfect, converting the soul;
The testimony of the Lord is sure, making wise the simple;

The statues of the Lord are right, rejoicing the heart;
The commandment of the Lord is pure, enlightening the eyes;

The fear of the Lord is clean, enduring for ever;
The judgments of the Lord are true and righteous altogether.

More to be desired are they than gold,
Yea, than much fine gold;
Sweeter also than honey and the honeycomb.

Moreover by them your servant is warned,
And in keeping them there is great reward.

Who can understand his errors?
Cleanse me from secret faults.

Keep back you servant also from presumptuous sins;
Let them not have dominion over me.
Then I shall be blameless,
And I shall be innocent of great transgression.

Let the words of my mouth and the meditation of my heart
Be acceptable in your sight, O Lord, my strength and my redeemer.

*L*ife. Have you ever tried to define it? Life is what happens to you while you are making other plans", said Balzer. "Life", says Biology, "Is the metabolic activity of protoplasm". "Life is 10 percent what you make it and 90 percent how you take it", said Irving Berlin. Someone has defined life as "A lot like tennis - the one who can serve the best seldom loses".

Philosophers and taxi drivers, artists and schoolteachers, scientists and politicians, you name them, people of every persuasion have tried to define the meaning of life. Buddhists, Communists, Democrats, Humanists, have all given their thoughts about existence and its meaning. Most begin by trying to understand life in terms of their own being and although it all seems brilliant, it is, in the end, speculative and very inadequate.

Here, in Psalm 19 is a totally different approach. It is called revelation. I like the way my friend Stuart Briscoe describes revelation. He imagines a child who finds a calculator in a field. He sits down under a tree and speculates about what he has found. He could think it is a bomb and if he presses a button and could throw it over there, he could blow up his school. That would be speculation but it would be inaccurate. He might think it is a dictionary that fell out of the sky and if he presses enough buttons he might learn to speak Martian. That's good speculation but it is wrong. But now along comes a man who says "Thank goodness you have found my calculator. I've been working on that thing for years. Here let me show you what it is and how it works". That will mean the end of speculation for the lad and the beginning of revelation."

The big question is, has the Creator of the Universe spoken? Has he revealed his plans and purposes in making this earth and those of us on it? The clear statement of this psalm is that he has certainly spoken and that everyone everywhere has an opportunity to hear him. C. S. Lewis called Psalm 19 the "Greatest poem in the psalter and one of the greatest lyrics in the world". Here is probably the fullest Old Testament statement of the doctrine of revelation. David sets out to tell us that God has revealed himself through three major media. First, to all humankind in creation (v.1-6). Second, to his people Israel in the law (v.7-10). Third, to the individual believer in experience (v.11-14).

Let's think, first of all about God's general revelation to everyone of us through the created universe. David is saying that no one can plead ignorance of God. Nobody is in such complete darkness that they have no glimmerings of light. Look at the sky, David is saying, it reveals God's glory and shows very plainly what he has done (v.1). Glory is the outward shining of the inward being of God. The sky shows God's glory continuously, day after day, night after night (v.2-3). Each day announces it to the following day; each night repeats it to the next. The message never stops, there is no intermission. From the heart of Vietnam to the heart of London as people look up to the sky and see the stars they are thinking God's thoughts after him.

It is true that God's revelation from the skies above us is a wordless revelation, it is a speechless, speech. Yet, there is a message. It is not just a meteorological message or a shepherd's indicator that "A red sky at night is a shepherd's delight or a red sky in the morning is a shepherd's warning". It is much more. The sky is declaring the glory of God, universally, "To the end of the world".

Now, David says, "Look at the sun". The suns witness is equally universal and equally continuous (v.4-6). God has pitched a tent for the sun to dwell in. It is the heavenly beduoin. Out emerges the sun from his tent like a bridegroom on his wedding day, or like an athlete on a running track. The language, of course, is figurative, this is not sun worship or star worship.

If I were to walk into your house I would know what kind of person you are by the kind of things you have in your house. So it is with God. God reveals himself in the visible works of his creation. The way day follows night, and Spring follows Winter all serve a common purpose to testify to the reality, power, goodness and wisdom of God.

What goes on even on earth, never to speak of the sky is a testimony to the glory of God. Did you know that an oyster lays 60,000,000 eggs a year. It has been calculated that if all the descendants of one oyster survived until it was a great-grandmother their shells would make a pile eight times the size of the earth! The humble mushroom, three inches in diameter, is even more spectacular, it drops 40,000,000 spores an hour and goes on until it has had 16,000,000,000 of them! Why, even the humble limpet amazes us. It takes a force 60 lbs per square inch to pull a limpet of a rock when it puts its foot down! When you dissect a limpet you will find a file about 2" long which works like a band-saw. Just feel the teeth on it. Limpets cut out a hollow in the rock with this file and however far they wander in search of food they always return to their hollow to rest! From limpets to stars, the creation of God is mind blowing.

I love the writing of Mark Twain and it seems to me Huckleberry Finn could have done with a good reading of Psalm 19! Huck had travelled down the Mississippi at night with negro Jim on a raft and described the experience perfectly: "It's lovely to live on a raft. We have the sky up there all speckled with stars and we used to lay on our backs and look up at 'em and discuss about whether they was made or only just happened: Jim, he allowed they was made but I allowed they happened. I judged it would have took too long to make so many. Jim said the moon could 'a laid them. Well that sounded kinda reasonable so I didn't say nothing against it because I'd seen a frog lay most as many, so of course it could be done and we used to watch the stars that fell too and see them streak down. Jim allowed they got spoiled and was 'hove of the nest!"

Yet, for all the glory of the heavens there is something missing in all this revelation. It is remote and vast and, even, vaguely disturbing. It makes you wonder and ask questions, but, it does little to warm your heart, allay your fears and calm you in your problems. Who doesn't identify with Chekhov when he writes in his story "Three years" of Laptev who is experiencing unrequited love? Yulia Sergeyevna doesn't respond to Laptev's approaches and Laptev takes leave of her and her father to walk home. Cehkov writes "All those lime trees, shadows, clouds, all those smugly indifferent beauties of nature seemed paltry to him now, as they always do when a man is dissatisfied and unhappy. The moon rode high in the heavens and the clouds raced swiftly under it. 'What a naive provincial moon, what pitiful wisps of clouds!', he thought."

Nothing, I find, can seem so indifferent to a breaking heart than nature. Don't you find the same?

So it is that God thankfully supplements his natural revelation with the second revelation to which we now come. This special revelation is found in a special revelation to a particular people through Moses and the prophets. It is preserved in Scripture. We move from the Divine name EL, God of Creation, to Jaweh, God of the Covenant. David has a very high view of Scripture. He uses six adjectives to describe the Word of God: "perfect", "trustworthy", "right", "radiant", "pure", "sure". He sees no flaw in them.

What a difference the Word of God makes! The Scripture makes "simple people wise". You can have a person who has tremendous knowledge of high finance or engineering or science. That person may make a lot of money but in the making of it may unmake their family, marriage, health and integrity. Wisdom is knowing what to do with what you have got. The Scriptures make simple people wise by teaching them what to do with their knowledge.

The Scriptures also "Rejoice the heart" (v.8). Few there are in the world who seem to realise what God's Word does for your joy. They think the Scriptures antiquated. The Scriptures "Enlighten the eyes" (v.8). Grown men and women who have never known them are exhilerated when they first discover the mines of wealth in God's Word. "The testimony of the Lord is sure" (v.7). God's Word is authoritative and gives direction.

Few would call the Scriptures "Sweeter than honey and the honeycomb" (v.10). The Devil wants us to think the world has all we need. Truth is, not since Manhattan Island was sold for $24 has there been so much dirt available for so little money as now. The Scriptures are so different. Did you ever get into what appeared to be the dry, dull pages of the revealed truth of God in Scripture and taste the sweetness? Did you ever come to its pages with fear and find peace? Have you ever come with guilt and found sweet forgiveness? Shall I ever forget teaching the truths of the tabernacle of the Old Testament one evening and seeing a young fellow, termed in those days a "punk", with his hair sticking up like a Mohican come running up to me shouting "I see it! I see it!!" By that he meant that he understood, at last, the way of approach to God, had come to Christ for salvation and had just been converted! Tabernacle teaching in those days was hardly considered the way to "Rap" with teenagers, I can tell you! No other book brings the wisdom of God on the one hand and the salvation of God on the other. It is sweeter than any honeycomb, indeed.

The psalmist has been generalizing; the sky, the sun, the law of the Lord have all been dealt with. Now he introduces himself, personally. "By them your servant is warned", he says (v.11). "Forgive my hidden faults" (v.12), he pleads. "O Lord, my strength and my redeemer" (v.14), he cries. Here is someone who sees God's glory in the skies, he delights in God's communications to people through the law but now everything becomes wonderfully personal.

There is such a thing as personal revelation. The Lord Jesus said: "I thank you Father that you have hidden these things from the wise and clever (intellectually arrogant) but revealed them to babes". Remember Peter the foul swearing fishermen of Galilee? You remember how he made such a great confession of Christ as the Son of the living God? Jesus immediately said "Flesh and blood has not revealed this to you but my Father who is in Heaven". Paul spoke about "The Son of God who loved me and gave Himself for me".

The revelation of God to David had very practical effects. He prays for santification, to be set apart for God (v.13). He wants to please God in every word he speaks and in every thought he thinks (v.14). He describes God as "my strength and my redeemer (v.14). No longer are we just thinking of an almighty distant creator, or even an awesome, dwelling-in-light-inaccessible law giver, we are thinking now about a God who comes so close that we can know him as our strength for just whatever faces us today. We can know him as the one who can redeem, buy back, all that has been lost in our lives that is truly and eternally worthwhile.

From making stars, one of the nearest of which is Sirius which is about 54 billion miles away, to forgiving sins and redeeming lives right down deep in our human communities our God is the God who has revealed himself. What a beautiful revelation it is. There lies the answer to all of our problems. God does not divorce nature from his Word, let us never do it either. See God's revelation to be a whole and flowing revelation through nature, the Bible and your human experience. Believe that revelation with all that it teaches and act upon it and you will truly become an integrated follower of Christ.

5

When You Just Cannot Find Happiness

Psalm 1

Blessed is the man
Who walks not in the counsel of the ungodly,
Nor stands in the path of sinners,
Nor sits in the seat of the scornful;

But his delight is in the law of the Lord,
And in his law he meditates day and night.

He shall be like a tree
Planted by the rivers of water,
That brings forth its fruit in its season,
Whose leaf also shall not wither;
And whatever he does shall prosper.

The ungodly are not so,
But are like the chaff which the wind drives away.

Therefore the ungodly shall not stand in the judgment,
Nor sinners in the congregation of the righteous.

For the Lord knows the way of the righteous,
But the way of the ungodly shall perish.

*I*t is a long time now since Professor Gallie of Queen's University's Philosophy Department asked me to write him a 3,000 word essay on the subject of happiness. Eagerly I began my research.

It seemed straightforward to me to begin my essay with the statement "Everybody is looking for happiness". When the Professor handed the essay back, I can still recall him looking over his half rimmed glasses and saying "Everybody is not looking for happiness. Some have given up". So much for my research!

What the Professor said is probably true but there must be very many people who long, deep in their hearts, to find happiness. Millions of people are pursuing it day and night and just cannot find it.

This first psalm is categorically stating that happiness can be found. The psalm begins with the word "Blessed" which can be translated "Happy". In Greek it means enriched, contented and fulfilled. In Hebrew the word is not found in the singular because in the Hebrew there is no such thing as a single blessing: wherever there is one there is another! There follows God's clear description of the truly happy person. You would think that the world would rush to read it and follow it but in fact they find it a real turn off. It isn't their idea of happiness and that is their tragedy.

The psalm doesn't mention the things most people think are an essential ingredient of true happiness. Hedonism - pleasure at all costs - is a high priority of many in the Western world. Yet this psalm doesn't mention laughter, comedy shows, alcohol, sex, entertainment, holidays, novels, films, food, creative work, decent housing, or anything the average person thinks will bring at least some measure of happiness or pleasure.

The psalm defines happiness by telling us, first, what happiness isn't! Most people reckon happiness depends upon good things happening to them. This psalm, and the Bible, shows that happiness is not necessarily related to happenings. You see, if happiness depends upon happenings and your happenings don't happen to happen, where are you? Again and again the Scriptures show us people who are in dark circumstances, yet happy! Paul sang praises with a bleeding back in a Philippian gaolhouse at midnight! Peter wrote of people knowing a joy unspeakable and full of glory despite the persecutions of Nero. Happiness is certainly more than the result of pleasant circumstances or personal possessions.

Who then is this contented, happy, fulfilled person? It is a person who does not walk in the counsel of the ungodly (v.1). Wherever happiness is to be found it will not be found in the maxims and laws of the ungodly. Another way to describe the ungodly is "Those who are loose from God". It doesn't just mean atheists and agnostics. It can just as relevantly describe people who refuse to give the Lord his supreme place in their lives, who refuse to regard God as God, even though they may give lip service to God. There is no happiness to be found in a Godless philosophy.

At Fremicourt in France two farm workers once came across a World War I artillery shell in a field. Like a fool one of them began hammering on it with the hope of salvaging the copper. Suddenly it exploded, killing one man and injuring the other. Isn't it terrible to think of a man hammering away on something that will destroy him? So are those who shape their conduct according to the plan or principles of the ungodly. True happiness is not found in that cul-de-sac.

It is not found in "the way of sinners" either (v.1). The Scriptures teach that a sinner is a person who "misses the target". It is a person who "misses the point" as far as truth is concerned, and "all have sinned and come short of the glory of God" (Rom. 3:23). Happiness will never be found "standing" in the way of sinners, nor "sitting in the seat of the scornful" (v.1).

To stand in the way of sinners is to identify yourself with what they do. To sit in the seat of the scornful is join those who blame everyone else but themselves for what is wrong.

That is the world's philosophy and it does not bring happiness. Meditate carefully on the three triple triplets in the first two verses of Psalm 1; "Walking, standing, sitting". "Counsel, way, seat". "Ungodly, sinners, scornful". It is the progress of evil, and each category moves to a climax. None of those climax's hold true happiness.

Does someone reading this study of the first psalm recognise that they have become a cynic? Have you become bitter in your life? Are you filled with self-pity? Are you hopelessly lost in the swamp of life? Do you just simply keep telling how wrong this or that was, or how rotten that person is to you, or how many promises they broke or how unfair life is? Would you like to replace stale cynicism with fresh hope? The answer lies right here in the very first psalm.

The happy person is actually able to reject the world's philosophy. How? By learning to "delight in the law of the Lord" (v.2). This is another name for the Scriptures. It includes the whole revelation of God. The truly happy person has discovered a completely different view of life in the Bible and believing it has driven cynicism away. It has given that person a completely different mind-set. Just as godless philosophy is doomed to disappointment, the opposite view leads to the opposite experience. The person whose delight is in the law of the Lord is totally different.

The law of the Lord, of course, shows us our sins but the Lord Jesus fulfilled that law and died for us and if we trust him as Saviour, then He will begin to impart the power into us to obey his law. He did not walk in the counsel of the ungodly, nor stand in the way of sinners nor did he sit in the seat of the scornful.

A man in Jerusalem once spoke to a gathering of Jews and Arabs. "Who is this happy man?", he said after reading Psalm 1. "Was it our great father Abraham?" "No", came the reply, "Because he told a lie about his wife". "Could it be Moses?" "No", said another, "He killed a man and hid him in the sand". "And", said another, "Lost his temper by the water of Meripah".

"Was it David?", "No!", they cried, "He committed adultery and slew Uriah".

"Well", said the man, "who is it?" An old Jew arose and said, "It is Jesus of Nazareth!" He had been a christian for some time and had not found the courage to tell others. Trusting that same Lord Jesus can bring that same happiness into your life.

The psalm is clearly teaching that the true believer is a Bible believer. Such a believer meditates in God's Word day and night. That doesn't mean they read the Bible all the time. It means that as they sit on a plane, or ride a bus, or walk on the street or work in a factory, lie in a hospital or whatever, the Scriptures are something they turn over in their mind. They delight in what the Scriptures say, they ponder it, love it, conform their lives to it. Their horizons are bounded by this revelation of God and his will. What criterion determines your behaviour? Do you ask advice of the ungodly or ask the God who has given us his advice in Scripture, or do you seek advice from the scoffers? It is a choice between human fashion and Divine Revelation.

The older I grow the more I am convinced that hidden in the Scriptures are priceless, verbal vaults. Silent. Hard to find, sometimes, easy to miss if you are in a hurry but there, awaiting discovery. God's Word stands ready to yield its treasures. Notice the effect of neglecting the Scriptures has had in one brief generation in our Western world.

What has happened to long-term marriage, child rearing, homosexuality, abortion, authority, integrity, individual fulfilment?

The New Age wave is certainly sweeping up our beach. People dissatisfied with the West's materialistic culture are turning to the East and back to pre-Christian beliefs and practices including spirit guides, pyramidology, tarot readings, crystal energy, fortune telling, and psychic discovery. 27 out of 100 adults in the UK now believe in reincarnation.

New Age influence is everywhere in our society penetrating the cinema, psychology, education, politics, business and medicine. The underlying beliefs of the New Age are capturing the minds of millions.

New Agers teach that each person is responsible only to themselves, not to a Creator God. "Right" and "Wrong", "Good" and "Evil" are merely illusions. Each person decides their own morality. Shirley Maclaine, Academy Award winner turned New Age high priestess says "There is one basic spiritual law which would make the world a happier and a healthier place and it's "Everyone is God. Everyone". What nonsense! Is there no limit to what people will do and teach when they ditch the Scriptures? The effects of such poison are catastrophic.

Do you want survival advice? Accept God's Word as just that. Meditate on and believe in the changeless, timeless truths of Scripture, otherwise you will be blown away. Only the believer is truly rooted in something which nothing can destroy. The result? "He shall be like a tree". Vitality. "Planted". Security. "By the rivers of water". Capacity. "That brings forth its fruit". Fertility. "In its season". Propriety. "Its leaf also shall not wither". Perpetuity. "And whatever he does shall prosper". Prosperity (v.3).

The psalm ends on a very serious note of warning. "The ungodly are not so", it says (v.4). There is a chill about those words. All the majestic themes that have been applied to the believer are shown to be irrelevant to unbelievers. They are likened to dead straw: chaff. That is about all they have in common. Trees are alive. Straw is dead. Trees have roots which are constantly nourished. Straw is uprooted corn. The wind drives the straw away. The water nourishes the tree. The contrast is between stability and instability, freshness and dryness, roots and rootlessness. They are two totally different qualities of life. So it is that the godly are rooted in God and are nourished by his Word. The ungodly are rootless and will not "stand in the judgment" (v.5). They will be condemned and kept apart from God's own people.

The psalm is certainly not saying that the ungodly do not prosper and grow rich and powerful in this world. Of course they do. The godly, by contrast often enjoy little prosperity and considerable affliction and oppression. But, it is a superficial prosperity which the ungodly have. It is extremely transient. It is happiness of a kind, it often gets them to the top and makes them highly successful but it is like a caterpillar which has no concept of a butterfly: the godless have no concept of what it is like to know God and the superior joy he gives. And the final judgment will show the difference (v.6). When the storm breaks, people's true identity will be revealed.

Going through a city in Eastern Europe recently I saw two words scrawled on the wall of a building. They said, simply, "No future". I wish I could have written another two words underneath, namely "Psalm 1". There is no more contemporary psalm in all the Bible. Let's heed it for it holds the secret of happiness.

6

When You Are Afraid

Psalm 27

The Lord is my light and my salvation;
Whom shall I fear?
The Lord is the strength of my life;
Of whom shall I be afraid?

When the wicked came against me
To eat up my flesh,
My enemies and foes,
They stumbled and fell.

Though an army should encamp against me,
My heart shall not fear,
Though war should rise against me,
In this I will be confident.

One thing I have desired of the Lord,
That will I seek;
That I may dwell in the house of the Lord
All the days of my life.
To behold the beauty of the Lord,
And to inquire in his temple.

For in the time of trouble
He shall hide me in his pavilion;
In the secret place of his tabernacle
He shall hide me;
He shall set me high upon a rock.

And now my head shall be lifted up above my enemies all around me;
Therefore I will offer sacrifices of joy in his tabernacle;
I will sing, yes, I will sing praises to the Lord.

Hear, O Lord, when I cry with my voice!
Have mercy also upon me, and answer me.

When you said, "Seek my face",
My heart said to you.
"Your face, Lord, I will seek".

Do not hide your face from me;
Do not turn your servant away in anger;
You have been my help;

Do not leave me nor forsake me,
O God of my salvation.

When my father and my mother forsake me,
Then the Lord will take care of me.

Teach me your way, O Lord,
And lead me in a smooth path, because of my enemies.

Do not deliver me to the will of my adversaries;
For false witnesses have risen against me,
And such as breathe out violence.

I would have lost heart, unless I had believed
That I would see the goodness of the Lord
In the land of the living.

Wait on the Lord;
Be of good courage,
And he shall strengthen your heart;
Wait, I say, on the Lord!

*F*ear comes in all sorts of ways. Many people are frightened long before their feet hit the floor in the mornings. Any one day could mean that you could be in an accident, be fired from a job, be the victim of a personal attack; you could be mistreated, robbed, slandered or threatened with a lawsuit.

About to speak to several hundred people one evening I gave them all a piece of paper as they came in. There were many furtive glances as to what this paper was for. They soon found out. I asked everyone present to write down a single problem that they had in their lives at that particular time. No names were to be written on the piece of paper, just a problem. I told them that I would read some of the contributions halfway through the service that evening.

When the time came, a very quiet hush fell over the crowd. I wanted, I told them, to prove that in what appeared to be an average crowd of people the problems hidden were greater than I realised. I wanted to show that I did not really know who I was talking to.

Let me share with you some of the things that were written on those pieces of paper that evening. The list was an eyeopener. "Broken marriage". "Recent death, after-effects on mother". "My organisation appears to be ruthless, uninterested in its individual members of staff and more inclined to expediency than integrity". "An alcoholic father". "Feeling distant from God". "Having a stammer which hinders freedom of thought and expression". "Brother doesn't speak to me, ever". "Lost my husband five years ago, am a widow with one son who can't get work ... I was stricken with polio when young and can't go to work. I can hardly make ends meet". "Brother on drugs, away from home". "Deep spiritual depression". "Compulsive gambling". "A constant barrage of immoral thoughts". "Leukaemia". "Isolation, I feel untouched humanly speaking by another living soul". "Totally out of the blue, a close relative was recently jailed for child molesting. I just can't believe it".

I could go on! "After 64 years worshipping in a certain church, I have been ostracised by many members". "The tension has become unbearable I have not the means to provide for my wife and four children". Do you blame me when I say that I still keep those pieces of paper to remind me that even smiling faces can hide incredible problems and unceasing fears? If these are but a few of the fears that are around in my neck of the woods, what about the problems of the world? From Sri Lanka to Zagreb, from the death squads of South America to the mafia in New York, from the killing fields of Cambodia to the hackings of South Africa, terrorism frightens millions.

What are we to say to the cyclones of Bangladesh or the earthquakes of California or Central Europe? What even of fears that people have of crowds or of enclosed spaces or even a trip to the dentists?! It all reminds me of a group of university students who once went for a fishing trip. They hired a boat and a reliable boatman to take them out on the bay. Without warning a storm broke and the old boatman sat with a worried look on his face. The students laughed at him in his fear and through their laughter declared: "We are not afraid!" The old man looked at them and said: "Yes, you are too ignorant to be afraid".

The writer of this psalm was certainly not too ignorant to be afraid. I thought about him recently when talking to a shepherd thousands of feet up on a mountain in Eastern Europe. He told me that he had lost two sheep in the night to a bear. As a lad David had known the attacks of lions and bears upon his flock. As a growing man he had been hunted for years by King Saul and his army. Saul even attempted to have David killed in his own bed. From the hatred of his own brothers to the awesome confrontation with the giant Goliath. David overcame fear. How? Through unshakeable, unbending confidence in God. Like a friend of mine in Peterhead in Scotland who was for many years the superintendent of a huge Church of Scotland Sunday School. She faced some incredible odds during her lifetime that would have frightened a lesser person. Long will I remember the little statement Bates used to encourage her supporters: "It's a lang time afore next Sunday and by faith we'll move mountains afore then". And, by faith, she did.

"The Lord is my light and my salvation, of whom shall I be afraid?", says David (v.1). As long as you have a light you can keep going in the dark. I once got lost while canoeing across a lake in New York State. I simply could not find my way back, because darkness had fallen and I had no light of any kind to guide me. I couldn't read the stars, being an Irish landlubber and I was afraid. Eventually the light of a distant shoreside building came in sight and guided me in. Are you ready for some light on your darkness? Your Lord is that light. He knows exactly where He is going. And why and for how long, and where to and who with. Even in death there is a valley of the shadow and you cannot have a shadow without a light, can you? In death as in life, the Lord is that light.

David also highlights the fact that the Lord is his salvation and this is a tremendous bulwark against fear. From v.4-6 he goes into the joys of a Jewish persons faith. He visits the temple and speaks of the symbolism of its structure. This brought him great joy. But it was inadequate, there was no sense of permanent atonement. Notice his lack of permanent assurance. Why do you think that was?

All over the world there are people who do not believe in eternal security. I know very well how controversial it all is but let me grasp the nettle. Think this through with me. Those Old Testament sacrifices could never purge the conscience of the worshipper. Never. Why? Because they had to be repeated. A sigh of relief went up from the Israelite when the sacrifice had been made. He could go out free. But suddenly, see him take hold of the priest: "But what happens priest, if I sin again, tomorrow? What then?" "Then you must come again with a sacrifice; a goat, a sheep or a few doves". "And if I sin again, next week? What then?" "Then you must bring yet another sacrifice. I am never finished with my work here. Have you noticed that there are no chairs here? Neither in the court or in the tent itself is there a single seat. There is no opportunity to sit or rest anywhere. I am not allowed to sit down at any time. I never finish. I never rest".

The forgiveness the Israelite received was only temporary and could never purge their conscience. "But", says Scripture of Christ, "This man after he had offered one sacrifice for sins forever, sat down on the right hand of God" (Heb. 10:12). There is no more sacrifice because their need be no more. When you rest in that finished work, permanent salvation is yours because it is a permanent work! If I thought I could lose my salvation then my peace with God would be shattered. "I give to my sheep eternal life and they shall never perish", says Christ. What a salvation! As Warren Weirsbe says in his excellent book "Meet yourself in the psalms", "No believer today need pray the prayer of verse 9 " ('Do not leave me nor forsake me, O God of my salvation'), because God has promised 'I will never leave you nor forsake you' (Heb 13:5). The fact of God's presence with us is assured by his promise, but the experience of his presence depends on how we relate to him in faith, love, obedience and desire. There is a difference in the christian life between 'union' (belonging to Christ) and 'communion' (enjoying fellowship with Christ)".

Aren't you glad, christian, that there is a New Covenant? The Old Covenant told Israel that if they kept God's law and followed him then he would bless them and keep them. If they disobeyed then God promised that he would scatter them to the four corners of the earth, they would no longer be his people and he would no longer be their God (See Hosea 1:8-10; Romans 9:25-33). The New Covenant is by far the better covenant because it is not based upon the blood of animals but is the New Covenant in Christ's blood. It does not depend on our keeping the law or any works of righteousness which we have done but "By grace you have been saved through faith and that not of yourselves it is the gift of God, not of works, lest anyone should boast" (Eph 2:8-9). Even when our faith weakens, he remains faithful. Peter's failure when he denied Christ did not land him in Hell. Christ's prayers for him made certain that his "Faith failed not". So it is that "He is also able to save to the uttermost those who come to God through him, since he ever lives to make intercession for them". (Heb 7:25)

It is Christ's present prayer life which saves your faith. Read the verse in Hebrews which I have just quoted again. Why is he able to save to the uttermost? Because he ever lives to pray for those who come to God by Him. No matter how dark the night, how bleak the day, how miserable your circumstances, christian, Christ, is praying for you. If that doesn't allay fear, what will?

Is it any wonder that David says in our psalm that he "Would have lost heart unless I had believed that I would see the goodness of the Lord in the land of the living". Believing in it he asks God to teach him (v.11), lead him (v.11) and to deliver him (v.12). It has been pointed out that it was possible when David heard of the death of his father and mother in the land of Moab (See 1 Sam 22:3) that, smarting under the experience and with a reference to the office of the "gathering host" in the march through the wilderness, whose duty it was, coming in the rear of the other tribes to take up and carry forward any sick or infirm folks who might have dropped from the mules or caravans without being noticed, David sang the sweet words of consolation put in his mouth by the Holy Spirit, "When my father and mother forsake me, then the Lord will gather me" (v.10). He will do the very same for you.

David's final call in the psalm is the best advice anyone who is experiencing fear could have. "Wait on the Lord: be of good courage, and He shall strengthen your heart: wait, I say, on the Lord" (v.14). The words are an answer to David's prayer, not merely an injunction to wait for an answer. He is saying the best policy in life is to wait constantly for the Lord because he will respond in the future as each crisis and need appears. With such a Lord go forward and face your fears with faith. The one finds it very hard to live with the other.

7

When You Need Forgiveness

Psalm 32

Blessed is he whose transgression is forgiven,
Whose sin is covered.

Blessed is the man to whom the Lord does not impute iniquity,
And in whose spirit there is no guile.

When I kept silent, my bones grew old
Through my groaning all the day long.

For day and night your hand was heavy upon me;
My vitality was turned into the drought of summer. Selah

I acknowledged my sin to you,
And my iniquity I have not hidden.
I said, "I will confess my transgressions to the Lord",
And you forgave the iniquity of my sin. Selah

For this cause everyone who is godly shall pray to you
In a time when you may be found;
Surely in a flood of great waters
They shall not come near him.

You are my hiding place;
You shall preserve me from trouble;
You shall surround me with songs of deliverance. Selah

I will instruct you and teach you in the way you should go;
I will guide you with my eye.

Do not be like the horse or like the mule,
Which have no understanding,
Which must be harnessed with bit and bridle,
Else they will not come near you.

Many sorrows shall be to the wicked;
But he who trusts in the Lord, mercy shall surround him.

Be glad in the Lord and rejoice, you righteous;
And shout for joy, all you upright in heart!

"*B*lessed is he whose transgression is forgiven, whose sin is covered. Blessed is the man to whom the Lord does not impute iniquity and in whose spirit there is no guile". Millions of people reading these opening words of Psalm 32 would give anything to be that person. Guilt brings people to the edge of despair in every society. It wrecks marriages, and brings mental and nervous breakdowns in its train. A lot of people live in dread of someone finding out their secret. They feel if people discover how bad they really are they will never be loved again.

I was told by a lady, once, how she had counselled someone who had been guilty of a certain sin. As it happened the lady had once committed the same sin and she shared the fact, in confidence, with her enquirer. The enquirer went and told others and they in turn snubbed the counsellor socially and personally! To such a counsellor I recommend this psalm. David never would have made the christian bookselling lists of our day. No christian writer would have dared to cover the detail of his sordid sin with Bathsheba and his consequent cruelty in the twelve months following his adultery. David would not have been allowed to stand before the "great congregation" of our day. Precious few would have forgiven him. But God told the story of his sin and his subsequent forgiveness for the whole world to read, and the adulterer and murderer's psalms are sung and loved the world over.

Sometimes when I see a man singing David's 23rd psalm with great fervour I wonder would he sing it so fervently if his daughter had been taken by David, or his son-in-law murdered by David or if his friend, Bathsheba's grandfather, had hung himself over David's disgusting behaviour? The Scriptures are extremely real and if you feel there is no hope for you, so bad is your sin, then study this 32nd psalm. Here is the exhilarating joy of forgiveness. The guilt ridden David ends up encouraging forgiven folk to shout for joy (v.11) and so can you.

David did not always shout for joy. For some considerable time David refused to confess his sin to God. He was downright stubborn. He wouldn't climb down. This did not help things one little bit. The better the man, the dearer the price he pays for a short season of sinful pleasure. When David took the city of Rabbah, at the very time he was refusing to confess his sin to God, he turned out to be extremely cruel with the people he conquered. He was so hard on other people when he should have been hard on himself. Outwardly he was heartless and cruel because of unconfessed sin but these verses tell us what he was like inwardly.

"When I kept silent, my bones grew old through my groaning all the day long. For day and night your hand was heavy upon me: my vitality was turned into the drought of summer" (v.3-4). Is there any better description of guilt? Vitality had gone. David's whole sensitive, tender, poetic nature had dried up. The musician in him was sapped, his open enthusiasm for life and all that was happening around him had been replaced with cunning and sullen duty. The Lord's hand was chastening him and he knew it. He was turned from a victorious leader into a cowering, dried up wretch. What the roaring, blasphemous Goliath couldn't do to him when he was a teenager, the giant lust had done to him in his fifties. How many more, like him, have known lust's sting?

The British newspaper "The Guardian" recently ran a survey to find out what women really think. Eleven thousand women responded and the survey found that of all respondents, 27% of married women had been unfaithful to their partners. Adulterers cannot be classified. The conscience lashed Puritan preacher is as likely a candidate as a Casanova. A business convention and a religious revival can both be occasions giving rise to the problem. The He-man Samson and the gentle poetic David both fell into lust's hands.

Why do people, in our generation as in David's, have affairs? Escape from life's pressures is one reason. Adultery seems to give a new freedom when as yet "There is no past to regret, no future to dread and no present sufficiently established to doubt". Boredom is another reason. A passive partner can also lead to adultery. In a world full of lonely people who are hungry for a sympathetic ear and a shoulder to cry on, sympathy can lead to tenderness and tenderness can lead to unfaithfulness in marriage. The passive partner can literally drive the other partner to adultery. Affairs, always remember, do not just begin for sexual reasons. They begin through resentments against insensitivity, excessive demands, neglect, lack of response and rejection.

With adultery, as with all other sin, there seems to be no tomorrow. The words of the popular song seem to be the general attitude: "Let the devil take tomorrow for tonight I need a friend". The sad thing is that the devil will not only take tomorrow, he will, step by step take your very life if you are not careful. Writers far greater than I could ever be have warned of the effects of David's particular sin. The most powerful story ever written, outside of the Bible about the effects of adultery was written by Tolstoy. Anna Karenina, his heroine fell into adultery's grip but Tolstoy, with incredible pathos, describes Anna at the end about to throw herself under the wheels of a train, almost as a universal warning against sins awful repercussions. "There", she said to herself, looking at the shadow of the truck on the mingled sand and coal dust which covered the sleepers. "There, into the very middle, and I shall escape from everybody and from myself!"

Who could not be warned against sins wages who has read Tolstoy's Anna's feelings and words seconds before she died? "A feeling seized her", writes Tolstoy, "like that she had experienced when preparing to enter the water in bathing, and she crossed herself. The familiar gesture of making a sign of the cross called up a whole series of girlish and childish memories, and suddenly the darkness, that obscured everything for her broke, and life showed itself to her for an instant with all its bright past joys. But she did not take her eyes off the wheels of the approaching second truck, and at the very moment when the midway point between the wheels drew level, she threw herself forward on her hands under the truck, and with a light movement as if preparing to rise again, immediately dropped on her knees. And at the same moment she was horrified at what she was doing. "Where am I? What am I doing? Why?" She wished to rise, to throw herself back, but something huge and relentless struck her on the head and dragged her down. "God forgive me everything!", she said, feeling the impossibility of struggling ...   A little peasant muttering something was working at the rails. The candle, by the light of which she had been reading that book filled with anxieties, deceptions, grief and evil, flared up with a brighter light, lit up for her all that had before been dark, crackled, began to flicker, and went out for ever."

When I read such moving writing I want to say to everyone on the edge of despair that they need not seek suicide as the way out. They will still have to meet God on the other side of death and to take your own life is murder just as much as it is taking someone else's. The message of Psalm 32 and of the whole Bible is that you can be forgiven by God, now.

How? Confession to God must come first. And it must come at a time when God "may be found" (v.6). It seems the emphasis is not so much confession to God in a day of grace but confession in a day of danger which might cut the person off from an opportunity to confess. That would seem to be the meaning of the phrase in v.6 which says "Surely in a flood of great waters they shall not come near him". Death can cut you off from the opportunity of confession and forgiveness. When Nathan the prophet confronted David with his sin, he wisely replied "I have sinned". That was the point that broke the deadlock. He did not wait a moment longer. "I acknowledged my sin to you and my iniquity I have not hidden. I said "I will confess my transgressions to the Lord" (v.5). Notice that David did not blame anybody else. It was "My" sin and "My" iniquity and "My transgressions. He confessed that he was wide of the mark (sin), he confessed that he was iniquitous (twisted), and that he was a transgressor (a rebel). He admitted that God was right and confessed that he was wrong.

David, in Old Testament days could not have been forgiven by God unless he had participated in heart and practice with the offering of a sacrifice for his sin. He calls the person "whose sin is covered", the truly contented person. God knows he tried in many devious and cunning ways to cover up his own sin with Bathsheba, even murdering Uriah her husband in the process (2 Samuel 12:9). He couldn't cover his sin before God, though. Neither can we. Where could he find a place where his sin could be covered now that it had been confessed?

If you had been in Israel in December 1854 and taken yourself down to the shores of the southern end of the Dead Sea you would have found a little, bearded man hunched over a canvas painting. In a wilderness of silica and limestone he worked with his gun at the ready, because of robbers. He had already risked his life to get there. For three or four days he and his guide had seen no sign of vegetation. At one point, he, the artist William Holman Hunt, had gone forward alone in search of a suitable sight for his painting and immediately sank into a pit of slime. Fortunately he had the presence of mind to throw himself down at once and literally crawl on his belly until he reached the safety of a firm ridge. By this means he literally saved his own life. What was the little man painting?

In a letter to the famous artist Millais, a few days earlier, Hunt described his purpose. "In Leviticus 16:20 you will read an account of the scapegoat sent away into the wilderness, bearing all the sins of the children of Israel, which, of course, was instituted as a type of Christ. My notion is to represent this accursed animal with the mark of the priest's hands upon his head, and a scarlet ribbon which was tied to him, escaped in horror and alarm to the plain of the Dead Sea and in a death-thirst turning away from the bitterness of this sea of sin. If I can contend with the difficulties and finish the picture ... it may be a further means of leading any reflecting

Jews to see a reference to the Messiah as He was and not (as they understand) a temporal king".

Hunt's painting "The Scapegoat" was hung on the line at the Royal Academy Exhibition of 1856. It was much criticised and misunderstood but Sir Robert Peel made an offer of 250 guineas for it. A man called Windus eventually bought it and I shall never forget the first time I saw it hanging in the Lever gallery at Port Sunlight. To a believer it is an awe inspiring painting for it beautifully typifies what happens to a person whose sin is forgiven and covered. On the great Day of Atonement the high priest "laid the sins" of the nation on the head of the scapegoat and the goat was taken away into the wilderness to be seen no more. When the Lord Jesus appeared on the banks of the Jordan what did John the Baptist say? He said "Behold the Lamb of God who takes away the sin of the world". Hunt caught the Bible's teaching, exactly.

Just as that scapegoat bore the sins of Israel, and even the sins of a David, away out of sight forever so the Lord Jesus on the Cross, bore our sins and to all who receive him as Saviour sin is no longer imputed. That means not only is the believers sin out of sight and covered forever but God does not even keep a record of it! To be quite honest with you, as I muse on this guilt erasing, sin forgiving, ever cleansing work of Christ on Calvary I can hardly sit at my desk! I want to get up and praise God all over again for such kindness to a sinful world and to a sinful person like me! I want to tell the Anna Karenina's of this world and all who are on the edge of despair to confess their sin, repent of it, and put faith in our Lord Jesus Christ. "For", writes Paul, "He made him who knew no sin to be sin for us, that we might become the righteousness of God in him" (2 Cor 5:21).

Did David escape the earthly consequences of his sin? Certainly not. The law of cause and effect applied to David as much as anyone else. There followed a chain of disaster. Bathsheba's little child died. Two years later one of David's sons treated his sister as David had treated Uriah's wife. Then Absalom murdered his brother and if David had punished Ammon for what he did to his sister the murder would never have taken place.   Why did he refuse to punish Ammon? The answer surely is that it is very hard to punish someone with a punishment you have sought to evade yourself.   David couldn't punish Absalom for his murder of Ammon, either, for the simple reason that he, David, had murdered Uriah.

David suddenly found that his privy counsellor Ahithophel had joined Absalom's rebellion. Why was that? Because the genealogical tables show that Ahithophel was Bathsheba's grandfather and that his son was Uriah's friend.   Soon virtually the whole nation followed Absalom and no event could have cut David deeper. He was thoroughly chastened by God.

Mark well the words of the godly F. B. Meyer: "Pain and sorrow may be devised against us by the malignity of an Ahithopel, a Shimei or a Judas: but if God permits such things to reach us by the time that they have passed through the thin wire of his sieve they have become his will for us: and we may look up into his face and know that we are not the sport of chance, or wild misfortune, or human caprice, but are being trained as sons. Without such chastisements we might fear that we were bastards."

Psalm 32 bursts into a song of deliverance and forgiveness on David's acquittal before God (v.6-7) but in the second stanza of the psalm the Lord talks to David rather than David talking to the Lord. He promises to guide him (v.8) I often think the promise "I will guide you with my eye" is like the look two people in love have, words are not necessary, at times. Yet the Lord warns David not to be obstinate. Bit and bridle are not meant to keep the horse from us but near us, so trials and disappointments should not keep us away from God but are designed to bring us near and keep us near (v.9-10).

The great psalm of penitence and forgiveness ends with a contrast between those who trust the Lord and those who don't. One has sorrows and the other mercies. So, "Be glad in the Lord and rejoice, you righteous: and shout for joy, all you upright in heart!". Seems to me if those who have been forgiven by God in Christ didn't have this holy hilarity, the very stones would cry out. Selah.

8

When You Are In Trouble

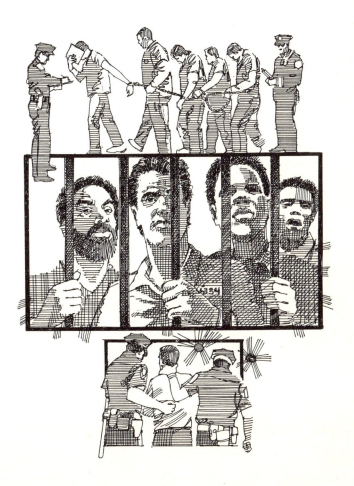

Psalm 46

God is our refuge and strength,
A very present help in trouble.

Therefore we will not fear,
Though the earth be removed.
And though the mountains be carried into the midst of the sea;

Though its waters roar and be troubled,
Though the mountains shake with its swelling Selah

There is a river whose streams shall make glad the city of God,
The holy place of the tabernacle of the Most High.

God is in the midst of her, she shall not be moved;
God shall help her, just at the break of dawn.

The nations raged, the kingdoms were moved;
He uttered his voice, the earth melted.

The Lord of hosts is with us;
The God of Jacob is our refuge. Selah

Come, behold the works of the Lord,
Who has made desolations in the earth.

He makes wars cease to the end of the earth;
He breaks the bow and cuts the spear in two;
He burns the chariot in the fire.

Be still, and know that I am God;
I will be exalted among the nations,
I will be exalted in the earth!

The Lord of hosts is with us;
The God of Jacob is our refuge Selah

*T*he ashen face of Mikhail Gorbachev returning to Moscow after being detained by the hardline coup spoke more than words can write. His trouble had brought him to contemplate suicide, he said, rather than give in to the coup. The gaunt face of John McCarthy returning from five years of kidnap in Beirut where things were so miserable in his dark environment that he stared for a whole day at a bowl of cherries before eating them, as it was the first colour he had seen in years, stirred millions. Trouble? We don't go looking for it because it comes looking for us.

Crises after crises is sweeping the world. In this year of writing we have known not only a Russian crises but India tettered on the brink of national disaster at the assassination of Rajiv Ghandi, the IRA tried to kill Prime Minister John Major and his Cabinet by firing a deadly rocket into Downing Street and a mountain in the Philippines, after a 611 year sleep, erupted angrily, spewing giant mushroom clouds laden with ash, steam and hot rocks. Hundreds of thousands were made homeless and many more thousands are living in fear of the dreaded mudflows which threaten to bury whole villages in the rainy season. Yesterday evening I dined in my favourite Chinese restaurant where the window near me had just been blown out by a bomb an hour earlier. In fact terrorists set up 40 bomb scares in my city yesterday afternoon. Trouble? It's epidemic.

Bank-fraud cases are usually dry tedious affairs, but not this year. Nothing in the history of modern financial scandals rivals the unfolding saga of the Bank of Credit and Commerce International. Never has a single scandal involved so much money, so many nations or so many prominent people. It is simply, to quote TIME magazine, "The largest corporate criminal enterprise ever". Countless people have had their funds wiped out.

No matter where you look today there is trouble. There is no section of human society that feels immune to trouble. Even Joe Roth, Chairman of 20th Century Fox says "I've been in the business for 18 years and I've never felt safe". Ned Tanen, a former studio executive said recently, "In Hollywood people wish you well only if they know you're terminally ill". It is a cut throat world from Hollywood Boulevard to Cullybackey, from Hanoi to Hammersmith, from the Kremlin to your own back yard. Is there, anywhere, a place of safety? If the song says "Nobody knows the trouble I've seen", can somebody tell us if there is a place of refuge from it all?

Let me answer that question by pointing out an interesting fact. It has to do with the Post Office in Jerusalem, which has a very famous department called the Dead Letter Department. What ends up there? Well, it seems that people all over the world who wish to reach God by mail simply address their letter "To God" and drop it in their local letter box. And where do their local post offices send such letters? To Jerusalem!

"The fact that tons of such letters accumulate every year", says Clive H. Rosen of the Judaica Philatelic Society, "shows that even if their politicians do not always recognise the Jewish State as the legitimate heir to biblical prophesy, and that Jerusalem will always be the seat of the God of Israel, their mailmen do. It also seems that postmen around the world are confident that the Israeli mailmen know where to deliver these letters. Some of the letters have a more detailed address, such as "God, the Western Wall, Jerusalem" or "Lord of the World, Seventh Heaven, Jerusalem".

It seems very clear that a lot of people feel there is something special about Jerusalem. They are right, of course. "The city of God" (v.4) has had a very special place in God's plans in the past and will certainly be very central to his plans in the future. Biblical prophesy shows very clearly that no matter what way world politics go, the ultimate battle for "Who rules?" will be fought in Israel and Jerusalem will be at the very centre of events. God, of course, does not now dwell there, the temple has gone, but the city, even at this stage in world events is never far from centre stage in world events.

The leading idea of Psalm 46 is the presence of the Lord in the midst of his city and people. This presence is the ground of their confidence. "God", writes the psalmist, "Is our refuge and strength, a very present help in trouble. Therefore we will not fear, though the earth be removed, and though the mountains be carried into the midst of the sea: though its waters roar and be troubled, though the mountains shake with its swelling" (v.-3).

We do not know for sure what the original context of this psalm was but it certainly fits the invasion of Judah by Sennacherib in the times of Hezekiah. The psalm metaphors and phrases resemble Isaiah's prophecies. When Hezekiah refused to pay tribute to Sennacherib "the Assyrian came down like a wolf on the fold". Jerusalem was surrounded and the foe demanded surrender. Suddenly, God intervened. "That night the angel of the Lord went out and put to death a hundred and eighty five thousand men in the Assyrian camp. When the people got up early the next morning they were all dead bodies!" Sennacherib withdrew and the people of God were rescued from their trouble.

Are you in trouble, today? Let God be your confidence. He is your strength and refuge. The proof of that for the psalmist was the recent deliverance enjoyed by the people of Jerusalem (v.4-7). "There is a river whose streams shall make glad the city of God", he says in v.4. The gentle flowing of the waters of Siloam are a real contrast to the raging nations outside Jerusalem (v.6). The city cannot fall because God is within her to protect and help her (v.5).

Of course Israel eventually turned away from God and broke the terms of her covenant with God. They reaped the sad consequences of their folly: eventually the city was left desolate, and the very temple fell. But the New Covenant, as I have tried to point out in this book before is so much better. Paul's superb utterance in Romans 8:31-39 is the New Testament counterpart of the great words of this psalm. There are no better words for a christian going through trouble to meditate upon. "If God be for us, who is against us?", writes Paul. It doesn't mean that we won't have trouble. It doesn't mean that illness and accident and unemployment won't come our way. The christian is not immune from trouble any more than a non-christian. What it does mean is that no opposition can finally crush us. "For us" is covenant language. It is God's undertaking to uphold and protect us as long as it is his will for us to stay on this earth and to finally lead us to the full enjoyment of himself. It doesn't matter what obstacles are thrown in our way, God will fulfil his promise.

J. I. Packer in his classic work "Knowing God" has pointed out that the translation "If God is for us who can be against us?" is wrong. The word should be "If God is for us who is against us?" Packer says what Paul is asking for is "A realistic view of the opposition, human and demonic, not a romantic pretence that it does not exist. Opposition is a fact: the christian who is not conscious of being opposed had better watch himself, for he is in danger. Such unrealism is no requirement of Christian discipleship, but is rather a mark of failure in it".

Paul continues to spell out the results of the New Covenant. "He who did not spare His own son, but delivered him up for us all, how shall he not with him also freely give us all things?" This is saying that no good thing will finally be withheld from us. We will never need more than God can supply and what God supplies will always be enough for the present. "Who shall bring a charge against God's elect? It is God who justifies. Who is he who condemns?" No accusation from anywhere or anybody can ever disinherit us from all that we have in Christ. If that fact isn't a hiding place in the day of trouble, what is?

Someone once asked the great evangelist George Whitefield what he would do if someone jumped up in one of his services and told the crowd that he was going to tell everybody about some very bad thing Whitefield had done in the past. Whitefield said he would tell him to tell the crowd the worst and then he would tell them that he knew of even worst things because he knew what the accuser didn't know, namely, he knew his own heart. When you come to know Christ as Saviour even your own heart's accusations cannot disinherit you of the forgiveness you have in Christ. "For", writes Paul, "I am persuaded that neither death nor life, nor angels nor principalities nor powers, nor things present nor things to come, nor height nor depth, nor any other created thing shall be able to separate us from the love of God which is in Christ Jesus our Lord".

The final stanza of Psalm 46 is declaring that the Lord shall finally be supreme over all nations (v.8-11). The way God has intervened to save Jerusalem is seen as a pledge and foretaste of the coming day when God shows himself to be the God who "Makes wars to cease to the end of the earth" (v.9). "He breaks the bow and cuts the spear in two: he burns the chariot in the fire", writes the psalmist. In days of trouble we must remember that God's promise is that the day is coming when "Out of Zion shall go forth the law, and the word of the Lord from Jerusalem. He shall judge between the nations and shall rebuke many people: they shall beat their swords into ploughshares, and their spears into pruning hooks: nation shall not lift up sword against nation, neither shall they learn war anymore" (Isaiah 2:3-4). This promise is etched on stone with a sculpture of a sword beaten into a ploughshare outside the United Nations headquarters in New York, but is it just a dream?

Certainly not. God is the guarantor of his promise. God calms his people with the majestic words "Be still and know that I am God. I will be exalted among the nations, I will be exalted in the earth!" (v.10-11).

The words run along the same channel as the words of Isaiah when he said "You will keep him in perfect peace whose mind is stayed on you because he trusts in you" (Is 26:3). How did you translate that verse into the Mbai language?", I asked my good friend Mr. Neville Taylor, veteran Bible translator and missionary to the Chad. "Well", he replied, "You know the expression in English which says when you are excited that "Your heart is in your mouth?" "I do", I replied. "Well I translated Isaiah's phrase as "You will keep his heart lying down whose mind is stayed on you". Lovely, isn't it?

To be still and know that God is God in the midst of trouble depends on one very vital thing: you must have confidence in him. Make no mistake that Satan is out to destroy your confidence in God. Did he not break Eve's confidence in God? Did he not call God's word into question? Did he not imply that God was a spoilsport, out to destroy any happiness they knew? Was not Adam sucked into believing Satan's lie? When the Lord Jesus, the second Adam from Heaven came was he not faced with the same Satan in the wilderness who tried out the same lie? All the business of tempting Christ to make bread out of stones and to cast himself down as some kind of circus trick, was it not an attempt to get Christ to break his confidence in his Father to feed him and to exalt his cause before men? If Christ's confidence in his Father had broken, the very world would have fallen apart. Why? Because, according to Scripture, by Christ all things consist.

Did Christ's confidence in his Father break? Never. He even went out towards the darkness of Calvary, singing. "And", writes Mark, "When they had sung a hymn they went out". To sing to his Father's glory before entering the greatest darkness and trouble anyone has ever known was confidence beyond measure. With such a confidence we are called upon to "Be still" and know that God is God. No wonder the people of God responded with the refrain "The Lord of hosts is with us: the God of Jacob is our refuge". If God could take a con-man like Jacob and make him a "Prince with God" (see Gen. 32:24) and be willing to call himself the "God of Jacob", he will bring us to the city which has a river, too. Trouble there will be extinct. Meanwhile, as my friend Mr. Taylor would put it, "Let your heart lie down!"

9

When You Are On The Edge Of Despair

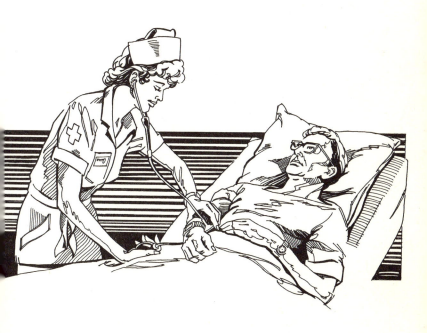

Psalm 88

O Lord, God of my salvation,
I have cried out day and night before you.

Let my prayer come before you;
Incline your ear to my cry.

For my soul is full of troubles,
And my life draws near to the grave.

I am counted with those who go down to the pit;
I am like a man who has no strength.

Adrift among the dead,
Like the slain who lie in the grave,
Whom you remember no more,
And who are cut off from your hand.

You have laid me in the lowest pit,
In darkness, in the depths.

Your wrath lies heavy upon me,
And you have afflicted me with all your waves. Selah

You have put away my acquaintances far from me;
You have made me an abomination to them;
I am shut up, and I cannot get out;

My eye wastes away because of affliction.
Lord, I have called daily upon you;
I have stretched out my hands to you.

Will you work wonders for the dead?
Shall the dead arise and praise you? Selah

Shall your loving-kindness be declared in the grave?
Or your faithfulness in the place of destruction?

Shall your wonders be known in the dark?
And your righteousness in the land of forgetfulness?

But to you I have cried out, O Lord,
And in the morning my prayer comes before you.

Lord, why do you cast off my soul?
Why do you hide your face from me?

I have been afflicted and ready to die from my youth up;
I suffer your terrors;
I am distraught.

Your fierce wrath has gone over me;
Your terrors have cut me off.

They came around me all day long like water;
They engulfed me altogether.

Loved one and friend you have put far from me,
And my acquaintances into darkness.

*S*ometimes I have the privilege of preaching in Edinburgh at Charlotte Baptist Chapel and I have on quite a few occasions had the privilege of bowing my knee in prayer with the elders of the fine fellowship of christians who meet at the Chapel. Rising from my knees in the vestry I have always cast a glance at a photograph which hangs on the wall there before going out to preach God's Word. The photograph is of Dr. Graham Scroggie, a former pastor at Charlotte Chapel.

Dr. Scroggie was a great Bible expositor and he had a little saying which I always carry around in my heart. He once pointed out that Jesus did not say "Feed my giraffes", he said "Feed my sheep". Sometimes those who teach the Scriptures do not put the hay down where the sheep can get at it, do they?

When you read Psalm 88 it is very hard to see where there is any feeding for anybody, especially for those who are on the edge of despair. Dr. Scroggie's famous book on the psalms has been a companion of mine for nearly 25 years and I have received great help from what he wrote about this psalm. He pointed out that this psalm has no parallel in all of the Psalter and is the saddest of all religious songs. Here the gloom increases as the psalm proceeds and its last word is "darkness". One thing is certain, if you are on the edge of despair, so was the writer of this psalm. You have a partner and it would be good for you to walk with him a little while. Walk with pleasure and you will soon find that he doesn't teach you half as much as you will learn when you walk with sorrow.

The psalm is divided into three parts. After calling upon God in the first two verses, the psalmist describes how pathetic his condition is. He certainly believes that it is God who has brought him to his miserable circumstances (v.3-8). In the second part he pleads with God to listen to him now or else it is a case of now or never (v.9-12). In the third part he wants to know why he has been brought to the edge of despair (v.13-18).

Maybe you can find parallels in your life with what this psalmist was experiencing. He says he has experienced affliction from his youth up (v.15). All his days have been a living death (v.3-6). Study the words he uses to describe his condition: he is "full of troubles" (v.3), he has no "strength" (v.4), he is "distraught" (v.15), his friends are "far from" him (v.8), he is an "abomination" to them (v.8). God has "hidden his face" from him and "cast him off" (v.14), he cries "day and night" and especially in the morning (v.1,9,13). There is no answer from anybody or anything to what he is going through.

Dr. Scroggie claims there is a strong case for this man having leprosy because mental anguish, or even soul distress would not make any one an abomination to his friends, nor necessarily isolate him from his acquaintances. He says that if we assume the psalmist had leprosy every line of the psalm becomes intelligible. Read the psalm again through the eyes of an Israelite who had leprosy. Do you remember the film "Ben Hur" and the story of his mother who was a leper? A leper in Israel was banished from home, no friends were allowed to approach, no attendance at Temple worship was allowed, and there was no known cure. Food taken to lepers had to be left at the entrance to some cave or other where the leper lived. The abyss of despair faced a leper, never talk of the edge of it.

Does some person read these lines and you have given up all hope? Maybe you have been disfigured in some horrific accident, maybe you are disabled by some incurable illness, maybe you lie paralysed like two ladies I know in Belfast who have been in the same hospital ward for 20 years. Despair is your constant companion, you go to sleep with thoughts of it, have nightmares because of it and waken to more of it.

This psalm is certainly the saddest of all psalms, it is certainly a psalm that many readers do not read as spectators but as participators, particularly with the mood of the psalmist. Yet, psalm of despair as it certainly is, it is not a psalm of utter despair. Shivers of light do appear and it is to those

that I direct your attention. For a start the very title gives light.
It tells us that this supposedly God-forsaken author seems to
have been one of the pioneers of the singing guilds set up by
David to which we owe the Korahite psalms, which are by
anybodys reckoning some of the richest in the Psalter. Even
though his life was a living death, it was not pointless.

What do you think life is all about? Making money? What
for? To buy food and clothes, or to go on holiday, or to buy
a nice home? Try telling that to a paraplegic lying on his
back. You'd be safer telling him there was no point in his
being alive at all because he can do none of those things you
think life is all about. There has got to be more about being
alive, even being just alive and no more, than making money
or home comforts. Surely the Scriptures teach that we were
created to love, worship and serve God. You can do that, no
matter what your condition. Even sickness can be to God's
glory as, for example, Job proved. Sin brought sickness,
sorrow and death into the world, but God's grace is such that
he can bring about good, not out of evil but in spite of it.

So, just as the psalmist's life, despite his desperate circumstances was not pointless, neither is yours, disability or not.
Even our very circumstances are not pointless. When Joseph
was thrown about by his brothers, cheated on and lied about,
he was eventually to say; "You meant it for evil but God
meant it for good". When the Lord delayed to come to the
disciples in the raging storm it was to teach them his power
over nature. When the Lord stopped to speak to the woman
with the haemorrhage on his way to see Jairus's dying
daughter, the news came that Jairus need not trouble the
Master further because the little girl had died; how do you
think Jairus felt, then? Did he despair? The Master delayed
to allow Jairus to discover that not only had he power over
disease but that he had power over death, itself. When Jesus
delayed to visit the dying Lazarus and then did not even arrive
for the funeral when Lazarus eventually died, Mary scolded
the Lord! Imagine scolding God for being late?! Jesus of
course delayed to show those sisters that not only had he

power over nature, or disease or death, but that he had power over decomposition. He raised Lazarus four days after he had been buried! God's seeming delays turn out to be eventual delights.

There is more than one shiver of light in this psalm of desperation. Not only is there light in its title, there is light in the fact that the psalmist prays at all! He prays in verse 1,2,9 and 12! In fact in verse 9 he says he prays "daily". Prayer is always a proof of lingering hope. You don't pray if you feel there is no hope left. It is also worth noting that the psalmist addresses the Lord, Jehovah, the covenant or promise making and keeping God, four times (v.1,9,13,14). His case might have been miserable but out there he knew there was a God who keeps promises. He was right.

This psalm has a desperate end but it does have a bright beginning. The psalmist addresses the God of his "salvation" (v.1). All over Eastern Europe we have "salvation" Fronts and committees trying to save their countries from economic and political disasters. God's salvation, though, is so different. In the Bible the word "salvation" is not necessarily a technical theological term but can simply denote "deliverance" from almost any kind of evil, whether material or spiritual. Theologically, however, it denotes the whole process by which people are delivered from all that interferes with the enjoyment of God's highest blessings and also describes the actual enjoyment of those blessings. It is fascinating to again realise that the doctrine of salvation in the Bible even extends beyond people to affect the whole universe. Eventually all things are to be subjected to the Son and all things in heaven and on earth will be summed up in Christ. No foe will remain to dispute Christ's authority or in any way mar the glories of His eternal kingdom. Salvation is a great word in Scripture and if you know it in your life let it cheer you, despite your present circumstances.

It could be that someone reading this psalm feels, like the psalmist hints, that their present circumstances are because they have sinned (v.7,16). Let us make a very clear distinction between penal punishment and chastisement in Scripture, especially in the light of the New Testament. For the christian the penal punishment for their sin is over. It happened at Calvary. The punishment you deserved for your sin fell on the Lord Jesus and you cannot be punished for it, ever again. The Lord can, of course, chastise us for our sins even as believers and use that to draw us back into his way, but, it is not penal punishment. You must never say when you are sick or ill or disabled or in financial trouble that the Lord is getting even with you. That simply is not true. He got even with you at the cross.

The last part of the psalm is really an unanswered cry, for the psalmist. "Will you work wonders for the dead? Shall the dead arise and praise you? Shall your lovingkindness be declared in the grave? Shall your wonders be known in the dark?", he asks. There is no immediate answer, but, of course, ultimately there is. The Lord will one day explain all that we have gone through but it is not guaranteed that we will have such knowledge during our lifetime. This psalm of desperation is a witness to the fact that unrelieved suffering may prove to be my lot on this earth, before I leave it. The same experience may be yours. When the Lord Jesus asks us to consider the birds of the air and how they are so free of anxious care it does not mean that little birds do not die of starvation or have accidents or experience, at times, unrelieved suffering. This psalm underlines this truth as graphically as anything I know.

Derek Kidner has said that although "darkness" is the final word of this psalm, "the happy ending of most psalms of this kind is seen to be a bonus, not a due: its withholding is not a proof of either God's displeasure or His defeat". Often for a believer the advantages in this world of belonging to the Lord are not patently obvious. It is the old question; "Can a person still have affection for God even if they seem to gain nothing by it in this world? It is a blessing that this psalm, depressing though it may seem to be to read, is in fact reminding us that the present world order is not the final one. The psalmist may end his psalm still in the dark and unrewarded but his existence "was no mistake: there was a divine plan bigger than he knew and a place reserved in it most carefully for him".

There is a way from dejection to joy. Out of narrow circumstances can come great blessing. This psalmist saw very little light, and I am not his critic, but, I would like to think that in all that he said there is more hope than he realised. There is only one psalm like this in the Bible in order to show the rareness of the experience dealt with, but there is one to assure all those on the edge of despair that God will not forsake them. Meanwhile, it's a bit like the story of the theological student who saw a youngster skiing with one ski, shortly after a snowfall. "Son, don't you know you are supposed to have two skies?" The lad looked up with a happy grin and replied, "I know I ought to have two, but I ain't got 'em. But, mister, you can have a lot of fun with one ski if you ain't got two". Indeed you can. Selah.

10

When Tongues Hurt You

Psalm 64

Hear my voice, O God, in my meditation;
Preserve my life from fear of the enemy.

Hide me from the secret counsel of the wicked.
From the insurrection of the workers of iniquity.

Who sharpen their tongue like a sword,
And bend their bows to shoot their arrows - bitter words,

That they may shoot in secret at the blameless;
Suddenly they shoot at him and do not fear.

They encourage themselves in an evil matter;
They talk of laying snares secretly;
They say, "Who will see them?"

They devise iniquities;
"We have perfected a shrewd scheme".
Both the inward thought and the heart of man are deep.

But God shall shoot at them with an arrow;
Suddenly they shall be wounded.

So he will make them stumble over their own tongue;
All who see them shall flee away.

All men shall fear,
And shall declare the work of God;
For they shall wisely consider his doing.

The righteous shall be glad in the Lord, and trust in him,
And all the upright in heart shall glory.

*T*he tongue is a fire. It is a world of iniquity. Go through the ten commandments and you will see that the tongue can be involved in breaking every one of them. "It is set on fire by hell", says the Bible. J. B. Philips translated that expression as the tongue making "the whole of life a blazing hell".

The tongue can certainly make mischief, and sometimes dangerous mischief. A woman's body was found floating in a river and on her person they found a note with two words written on it: it read "They said". What "they" say can be extremely hurtful, can't it? "I hear Tom and Jane are getting divorced ... they say she was unfaithful". "I hear she's a flirt, watch out for her". "Word has it that they had to get married". "Oh, Jimmy? He's a bit odd, they say".

The tongue is humanly untamable. We train seals to carry balls on their noses, tigers to jump around stools in a circus ring, killer whales to carry humans on their backs, alligators to turn over and get their stomachs rubbed, pigeons to carry our messages, and, I've even seen parrots trained to ride on roller skates. But no person can tame the tongue. It's power can wreck marriages, divide professional business people, split churches, and even set nation against nation in war. The hurtful power of the tongue can keep you awake long into the night.

It had certainly been hurting David. In the opening words of Psalm 64 he speaks of a crowd of detractors who have been sharpening their tongue against him "like a sword" and who bend their bows to shoot their arrows, arrows that are "Bitter words, that they may shoot in secret at the blameless: suddenly they shoot at him and do not fear" (v.3-4). David is not saying that the blameless are sinless but he is saying that they are not guilty of the things this crowd are saying about them.

Maybe you are in the very same position. Tongues have been lashing you of late accusing you of things you have never done or even thought of doing. Those tongues have brought you to the edge of despair. It is the boldness of these people that worries you, isn't it? They are very clever in their schemes, extremely inventive and persistent. They were the very same in their scheming against David. "We have perfected a shrewd scheme", they boasted (v.6), they talked of "laying snares, secretly" (v.5). Of course, all the time they were convinced that no one saw what they were doing, not even God (v.5).

There is a document in a British court of law called a Crime Sheet which lists the cases to appear before a magistrate. It contains the names and addresses of all the accused and lists their alleged crimes. On the biblical crime sheet the tongue is one of the accused and the list of offences is enormous: dishonesty, unkindness, flattery, impurity, blasphemy, pride, criticism, exaggeration, temper, greed, slander, boasting. David faced the full blast of the crimes of the tongue but the heartening thing about his psalm on the hurtful tongue is the fact that he knew of a principle in life which is always at work despite the tongues power. It is the principle of the retribution of God. Let's think about this principle.

David took the "arrows" (v.3) of the enemies tongue but it only took one of God's arrows to down the enemy (v.7). The tables suddenly turned. What they intended to inflict on others fell on themselves. This psalm was once captioned "The boomerang of malicious speech". It is a clear case of God's retribution. It is true that the doctrine of God's retribution is frowned on by many in our modern day but the Bible clearly teaches it. Of course there is forgiveness for those who repent but there is Divine retribution for those who don't. If there wasn't, Heaven would turn black.

Why is it that we shy away from the truth of God's judgment on sinners? In a world that sells itself to the gods of greed, of envy, of violence, of immorality, of self-will, the church tells people of God's kindness but says hardly anything of God's judgment. It seems to be a taboo subject in our society. It is anything but taboo in the Bible. There are more references in the Bible to the wrath and judgment of God than there are to his love and tenderness. The Bible says God will "pursue His enemies into darkness" (Nahum 1:2-8) and Paul says that the Lord Jesus will one day appear "In flaming fire taking vengeance on those who do not know God and on those who do not obey the gospel of our Lord Jesus Christ" (2 Thess 1:8).

Perhaps our thinking is clouded by the fact that we think God's wrath and retribution suggests cruelty. It doesn't. It is judicial, it is the wrath of a judge. If someone came down the road in their car, driving stupidly at breakneck speed and killed your daughter, would you demand justice? Would you be angry at the driver? Of course you would demand justice and of course you would be angry. If you weren't there would be something desperately wrong with you. So, what kind of God would God be if he did not judicially deal with David's slanderers? What kind of God would God be if he did not deal with those tongues that are piercing the very soul of your family? He would not be God at all.

God's wrath and retribution is something people choose for themselves. If people rejected God's mercy and forgiveness in Old Testament days and reject the light that comes to them through the Lord Jesus in the New Testament, they must bear the consequences. As J. I. Packer says "All that God does subsequently in judicial action towards the unbeliever, whether in this life or beyond it, is to show him, and lead him into the full implications of the choice he has made. In the final analysis the essence of God's action in wrath is to give people what they choose. So the good news is that if people repent and receive the Lord Jesus as Saviour they will be "saved from wrath through him." If they don't, they won't.

When God intervened and brought his retribution on those who used their tongues in a hurtful way on David, the effect was so striking that "all who saw them shuddered" (v.8). David teaches that that will always be the result. "So", says verses 8-9, "He will make them stumble over their own tongue: all who see them shall flee away, all men shall fear". This is teaching that people will be in awe of God when they see his retribution at work. Is there not comfort in this for you? Harassed as you might be with all the wicked things your enemies are saying against you, when those enemies stumble over their own tongue for all to see it will cause people to see that neither God nor his people are mocked without the mockers reaping what they sow. Those who look on, David says, "shall declare the work of God for they shall wisely consider his doing" (v.9). That means people will gain an insight into how God works.

Look at the insight we have all gained into God's ways through the slander of Pottiphar's wife on Joseph. Did any court of law vindicate Joseph during his lifetime for the rotten slur the subtle and wicked woman cast on Joseph's character? Who vindicated him? God did, and people through the ages have gained incredible insight into God's ways because of the way God did it. The same applies to the plotting and lies that Joseph's own brothers executed against him. When they "bowed down before him to the earth "after his exaltation to the echelons of power in Egypt it was a different story. Why, it even "Pleased Pharaoh and his servants, well" (Gen 45:16). Do you see the principle? When slander is retributed by God's intervention, our psalm tells us "All men shall fear".

Who in all Scripture experienced this principle more than David, himself? Some say that Saul probably tried to kill David at least thirty times. Called for everything, hunted like an animal by Saul's army for years, David never lifted a finger to bring retribution on Saul. When the retribution came it was devastating. Saul who tried to pin David to the wall with a javelin committed suicide and the Philistines pinned Saul's body "to the wall of Beth Shan".

I often think of Nabal, a wealthy sheep owner at Carmel, in Israel. When David was on the "run" from Saul he and his men showed great kindness to Nabal's shepherds. One day David sent ten young men to ask Nabal to "Please give whatever comes to your hand to your servants and to your son David" (1 Sam 25:8). It was a reasonable request but it got an unreasonable answer. "Who is David, and who is the son of Jesse? There are many servants nowadays who break away each one from his master", answered Nabal. "Shall I then take my bread and my water and my meat that I killed for my shearers and give it to men when I do not know where they are from?" It was a case of the hurtful tongue, indeed. Nabal was accusing David of breaking away from a master who if he had seen David, even in his bed, would have killed him immediately (See 1 Sam 19).

David reacted with fury. He took 400 of his men and descended upon the house of Nabal to kill him and every male within his household. Suddenly as he came down the road to Nabal's place he met a fascinating sight. There in front of him was a beautiful woman, down on her knees on the ground. She was Nabal's wife and her speech to David is a classic example of the very thing he is writing about in this psalm:

"Please", she said, "let not my Lord regard this scoundrel Nabal. For as his name is, so is he: Nabal is his name and folly is with him ... since the Lord has held you back from coming to bloodshed and from avenging yourself with your own hand, now then, let your enemies and those who seek harm for my Lord be as Nabal ... for the Lord will certainly make for my Lord an enduring house, because my Lord fights the battles of the Lord ... yet a man has risen to pursue you and seek your life, but the life of my Lord shall be bound in the bundle of the living with the Lord your God and the lives of your enemies he shall sling out, as from the pocket of a sling". David wisely listened to Abigail's advice and put his sword away. The next morning Nabal had a heart attack and ten days later, Nabal was dead.

If the principles of God's retribution against God's enemies was true in David's life, think of it in all the host of characters on the pages of Scripture: Moses, Joshua, Deborah, Gideon, Samson, Isaiah, Daniel, Paul, Peter, etc. It is a study worth following and in all cases, let me state it again, those who looked on gained insight into how God works.

What does it all mean to a believer, though? David gives us the answer. "The righteous shall be glad in the Lord and trust in Him. And all the upright in heart shall glory" (v.9-

10). David rises from his own particular case to the universal operation of righteousness. No matter what your enemies may throw at you, christian, you have nothing to fear. To all that goes on around you there is only one answer, "Hide in the Lord" (v.2) and what begins in gloom will end in glory. It is guaranteed. Does that not bring you back from the edge of despair when the hurtful tongue is breaking your heart? If it doesn't, what will? Meanwhile, heed the words of William Cowper:

> *"Assail'd by scandal and the tongue of strife,*
> *His only answer was a blameless life".*

11

When You Are Building

Psalm 127

Unless the Lord builds the house,
They labour in vain who build it;
Unless the Lord guards the city,
The watchman stays awake in vain.

It is vain for you to rise up early,
To sit up late,
To eat the bread of sorrows;
For so he gives his beloved sleep.

Behold, children are a heritage from the Lord,
The fruit of the womb is his reward.

Like arrows in the hand of a warrior,
So are the children of one's youth.

Happy is the man who has his quiver full of them;
They shall not be ashamed, But shall speak with their enemies in the gate.

*T*here are few people in this world haven't experienced the messy disturbance building can bring. Whether it is a new front porch or a new kitchen, whether it is a new roof or a new house, building spells hassle. Disturb any wall in your house and grit will even get in your toes at bedtime! Building is messy, full of problems and challenges and, if you are not careful, can bring disaster when things go wrong. As they say in America "When you are up to your eyes in alligators it is hard to remember that the original intention was to drain the swamp". Building is not all that much different. It seemed a good idea at the time!

Building families and communities brings its pressures too. Watch any young couple starting out on life together. While their relationship is new, it sparkles. Soon, however, problems come and pressures come which they never even dreamt about. Millions of them opt for the architects blueprint which says you don't have to torture yourself, just bail out. Try an exciting affair, we are in the nineties now, not the 30's. Why, in a jewellers shop window some time ago there appeared the sign which read "We rent wedding rings!" Needless to say the building of families is falling apart all over the nation.

Look at the situation regarding building communities. A current example is the Soviet Union. Suddenly, the old Soviet Union is gone. As I write the Soviet Union's death warrant was signed by the country's supreme legislature yesterday, paving the way for a new looser confederation of sovereign states. They haven't even got a name for it, yet. Among those names being discussed are the Union of Sovereign Soviet States, the Euroasian Economic Community and the Commonwealth of Sovereign States of Europe and Asia. One cynic even suggested the Club of Crippled Nations. The huge blob of blood red that dominated maps of the Euroasian landmass for 70 years is now broken up into a crazy quilt of squirming lines enclosing a kaleidoscope of colours. The White House band is certainly going to have to learn a lot of new national anthem tunes to play for visiting presidents in the next few years! A western christian leader who talked to Boris Yeltsin and Mikhail Gorbachev shortly before the botched coup, returned from the Soviet Union and passed the word to the American President, George Bush that both men had told him of the need for "some philosophy, some religion, an inner strength" for their society. They are in a state of "transitional rule" but the world wants to know the answer to a huge question: a transit to what?

Building villages, towns, cities, nations or families is not easy. There is, though, no better advice any person, community or nation could take than the advice of Psalm 137. It is called "A song of Ascents" and is said to be for, or by, Solomon. Nobody had more experience of building than Solomon, particularly when he built the temple in Jerusalem on Mount Moriah. He contracted with the king of Tyre for the supply of cedar and cypress wood and arranged for Phonecian builders to supplement the Israelite corvee.

Solomon's temple was finished in seven years and his palace in thirteen years. In all a great amount of bronze was used for ornamental work and for architectural features. It is only in comparatively recent years that the great mining and smelting enterprises of Solomon have become known for they are not referred to in the Bible. Solomon's work of building extended throughout the land. He built at Gezer, Hazor, Megiddo, Tadmor, Upper Beth-horon, Lower Beth-horon, and in Lebabon. He did additional building at Jerusalem. He made store-cities and cities for his chariots and cavalry throughout the domain. He had 1400 chariots and 12,000 horsemen and 4,000 stalls for his horses. He was inconceivably wealthy.

The underlying theme of this five verse psalm is the utter uselessness of all human effort which does not rely on the will, power and goodness of the Lord. "Unless the Lord builds the house, they labour in vain who build it: unless the Lord guards the city, the watchman stays awake in vain", writes Solomon (v.1). Building without God is folly. The men of Babel soon found that out. Did not the Lord Jesus warn that is possible to go to a lot of effort in life to build something and then to discover that it is all in vain because it has been built on sand?

Could it be that you are on the edge of despair because for years you have not been building on the right foundation? A lot of people have got there. Take Jack London, the American novelist and short story writer. A self-made man, London became the highest paid living writer in history, the world's first millionaire novelist. His most famous novel "The call of the wild", the story of an Alaskan wolf, has recently been made into a film ("White Fang"). London remains, today, one of the most popular writers in the world: his novels and stories have been translated into over forty languages. Yet, this brilliant writer wrote, "I believe that life is a mess ... it is like yeast, a ferment, a thing that moves and may move for a minute, an hour, a year, or a hundred years, but that in the end will cease to move. The big eat the little that they may continue to move, the strong eat the weak that they may retain their strength. The lucky eat the most and move the longest, that is all". On November 22nd 1916 he was discovered comatose on the floor after apparently injecting himself with an overdose of morphine. He was forty years old.

See what I mean? Life without God is meaningless and miserable and ultimately hopeless. If you have lived your life up to this time without God then repent of your sin, accept the Lord Jesus as your personal Saviour and start building your life on the proper foundation. No wonder your life is lonely, you neglected to bring God along with you.

Houses make cities and "Unless the Lord guards the city, the watchman stays awake in vain". This is not preaching laziness masquerading as religious trust. For example we owe a tremendous debt to many of our schoolteachers who do a tremendous work amongst the children of our cities and towns. We owe debts to our emergency services, to fire authorities, to ambulance drivers, to policemen, to visionary city fathers who inspire with their leadership. This nation owes a great debt to its army and air force and navy which protects its interests. What the psalm is saying is that all guarding and caring and work to help is in vain without God's blessing. It is not work but self torturing care and work which does not seek God's blessing that is designated by the psalmist as vain. Let us never imagine that our social and civic life bears no reference to God. I stood in Lenin's mausoleum in Moscow, once, and gazed at what is purported to be his embalmed body. His vicious and godless ideas have crumbled with the summer of '91. I visited Christ's mausoleum in Jerusalem and when I got there I found a sign on the door. It read "He is not here. He is risen". The contrast between the two was glorious. Glasgow's motto was "Let Glasgow flourish with the preaching of the Word and the praising of his name", now it simply reads "Let Glasgow flourish". The Glasgow city fathers would do well to read our psalm and reinstate their full and ancient motto. Would to God such a motto were the motto of every city and nation in the world.

The psalm now turns to the individual. "It is vain for you to rise up early, to sit up late, to eat the bread of sorrows: for so He gives his beloved sleep" (v.2). The psalmist is saying that long hours do not mean prosperous work. Some of the saddest cases, even in our modern workaday world are the workaholics. Often their lives are frustrated by the consequences of high-pressured competition. In the process of becoming "successful" their relationship with their families are completely eroded. They live like a crowd of strangers under the same roof. They serve a very cruel master called "success at any price".

So, what's the answer? Quit? Drop out of responsible living? That would be very foolish. The psalm is telling us that the great gains in life are not secured by relentless work, by rising up early and sitting up late but by honest work balanced by proper rest, all done in dependence and trust in God. Solomon put it very clearly when he wrote "The fool folds his hands and consumes his own flesh. Better is a handful with quietness than both hands full, together with toil and grasping for the wind" (Ecc 4:5-6). A free translation of that verse reads "One hand full of rest is better than two fists full of labour". Again in the Proverbs Solomon wrote on the same theme; "Better", he wrote, "Is a little with the fear of the Lord than great treasure with trouble" (Prov. 15:16).

If we live in the fear of the Lord, then our lives, even our working lives will be balanced and the result will be that the Lord will lift away anxious care from us and we will sleep in our beds at night. If we live according to God's laws our conscience will be clear and sleep will be easy. It is interesting to remember that it was in sleep that God gave Solomon his greatest gift, the gift of wisdom (See 1 Kings 3:5-14).

The final section of the psalm is about the family. "Behold, children are a heritage from the Lord, the fruit of the womb is His reward. Like arrows in the hand of a warrior, so are the children of one's youth. Happy is the man who has his quiver full of them: they shall not be ashamed, but shall speak with their enemies in the gate" (v.3-5).

There are four things said about children here. First, they are a gift from God. That means they belong to him and they are only loaned to those who have them. They are not ours to keep. Let's never forget that. Second, they are his reward. That does not mean if you are a childless couple that the Lord has not rewarded you. He has rewarded you in other ways. But, if you have children then they are assigned to you by God as a reward. Third, children are as "arrows" (v.4). That means they come with different inclinations, fulfil different uses. For example we have twins in our home. To say they are alike is an understatement, and this was especially true when they were babies. In fact when they were babies, one of them took ill and their mother suddenly discovered herself starting out for the doctors with the wrong baby! Twins and all as they are, though, they are two very distinct individuals.

If God has placed into your quiver the arrows of children

then God will give you the wisdom to launch them out on life, equipped to fulfil God's purposes for each one of them. People with a family behind them are not ashamed to speak with their enemies in the gate, says verse 5. It truly is a lovely thing to have a family to come home to when even the whole world seems to come against you. Let us as parents bend those arrows in our quiver towards the things of God and his Word because the arrows in our hands will very soon be out of our hands and then it is too late to bend them. Even if these arrows in the hand prove to be an arrow in the heart and a constant grief in later life, at least if we have sought to bring them up in the nurture and admonition of the Lord our conscience will be clear and the responsibility of what they do with what they have learnt about God will be theirs. Even as I write these words my mind is flooded with the memory of my godly mother, (my father died when I was but seven), and I thank God for her constant vigil over my life to bend me towards the Lord Jesus and the things of his kingdom. The Lord guide all of us to raise our children to his glory.

So, the little psalm teaches us that whether it be houses, cities, or families we are building, if we want to be successful then we must recognise the Lord in everything we do. The result will be inevitable blessing. We must use everything as if it belongs to God. He gives us wheat, but we must bake the bread. He gives us cotton but we must convert the clothing. He gives us trees but we must build our homes. He provides the raw materials and expects us to make the finished products with them. Let's go to it!

12

When You Can't Sleep

Psalm 4

Hear me when I call,
O God of my righteousness!
You have relieved me when I was in distress;
Have mercy on me, and hear my prayer.

How long, O you sons of men,
Will you turn my glory to shame?
How long will you love worthlessness
And seek falsehood? Selah

But know that the Lord has set apart for himself him who is godly;
The Lord will hear when I call on him.

Be angry, and do not sin.
Meditate within your heart on your bed, and be still. Selah

Offer the sacrifices of righteousness,
And put your trust in the Lord.

There are many who say,
"Who will show us any good?"
Lord, lift up the light of your countenance upon us.

You have put gladness in my heart,
More than in the season that their grain and wine increased.

I will both lie down in peace, and sleep;
For you alone, O Lord, make me dwell in safety.

*M*illions of people go to bed on vallium every night. Drugs to induce sleep are a priority for too many people. A lot of insomnia comes from too much rushing around, too many deadlines, and far too frantic schedules. People every-where gobble down food and are raked with indigestion. Natural, peaceful sleep is only a pipe-dream, if you will excuse the phrase. Psalm 4 tells us that how we sleep at night will all depend on how we live our day. Two lifestyles show themselves in stark contrast in the psalms.

After calling on the God who has shown him past mercy (v.1), David speaks of the fact that people will always seek what they love (v.2). It worries David that so many people love worthlessness and seek falsehood. He wonders how long it will all go on. Let's let the truth of what David is saying search us. He is saying that we get exactly what we go in for. If we seek a godly lifestyle, we will get it. That doesn't mean we have to go around like an unmade bed all day, dipped in dettol. It means that our hearts and our lifestyles will be set apart for God, for, says David, "The Lord has set apart for Himself him who is godly" (v.3). When you have lived a day which is, in its motivation and behaviour, set apart for God, your conscience will not begin eating away at you when you lie down to sleep.

"Be angry, and do not sin. Meditate within your heart on your bed, and be still. Selah", says the Greek version of verse 4. If we all followed this excellent advice then we would find that when we reviewed the day, in our minds at night, sleep would soon come. All anger is not sin. In fact anger is a God-given emotion. The Bible does not teach that we should never be angry. David is warning us, though, to give no opportunity to the Devil when we are angry. Uncontrolled anger is a wide open door for Satan. He will enter it every time and set to work replacing his character and his witness for that of Christs.

It is perfectly justifiable, for example, to be angry when God's word and will are constantly disobeyed. We are to be angry but not to carry anger to the point of its becoming sin. Paul once wrote that we are not to "let the sun go down on our wrath" (Eph. 4:26). One thing is certain, Paul was not saying that we are to be angry until sunset, for then our wrath might lengthen with the days and people in Greenland where days last beyond a quarter of the year have plenty of scope for revenge! No! The apostle's intention, as was David's, was to warn us against nursing resentment and to make sure we draw a firm line between righteous and unrighteous anger. Satan obviously loves to lurk around angry people, hoping to be able to exploit the situation to his own advantage by provoking them into hatred or violence or a breach of fellowship. If this happens in your life sleep will truly elude you.

Grumblers, of course, have few sweet dreams. "There are many who say 'who will show us any good?'", say the grumblers (v.6). Some people are born pessimists. They always see the dark side of things rather than the bright. An optimist may be wrong as often as a pessimist but the optimist is far happier. Grumbling reveals a lot about us. It is serious not only because God hates it but because it reflects what lurks in our minds and hearts. Always remember what Samuel Johnston said; "The usual fortune of complaint is to excite contempt more than pity". When you are grumbling and bitterly complaining it might be pleasing you to "get it off your chest" but it is not necessarily pleasing those who are listening to you.

Murmuring leads to discontent. Discontent leads to covetousness and covetousness is a sin. Think of Ahab in Scripture, or, the disciples in the Upper Room or Judas complaining of Mary's kindness to Jesus. Murmuring is a furtive thing, hiding deeper things. Abraham Lincoln, long before he became U.S. President was once passing a neighbour's house and his two small sons were arguing. "What's wrong?", asked the neighbour. "Just what's the matter with the whole world", answered Lincoln, "I have three walnuts and each boy wants two".

There is no doubt that much of our local, national and international tensions and divisions come from a grumbling spirit. It would be much better if we had Paul's spirit when he said "I have learned in whatever state I am, to be content" (Phil. 4:11). All across the world people will toss and turn on their beds tonight because of the worry and stress caused by having too much while others who have few material possessions have a cheerful and contented spirit. If you doubt me, ask Sir John Paul Getty, a most generous man, who has the burden of earning £3 every second! You may say that I am crazy to use the word "burden" but I would remind you that Sir John once said "Money does not bring automatic happiness. There have been many times when I have cursed it!" The Hon. Mrs. Charlotte Morrison, said to be the second richest woman in the United Kingdom, now sadly divorced, said recently "Sometimes I think, 'Oh! I'd love to talk to somebody or I wish there was somebody here'". All around us we see the truth of the Saviour's words, "A persons life does not consist in the abundance of the things they possess".

Let us always remember that money can buy us a bed but it cannot buy us sleep. Godliness with contentment is great gain and it is a first rate tonic for a peaceful night. Pity the people whose peace is dependent on plenty who, unless they have corn and wine are not glad. If your joy is earthbound it will not rise above earthly things but if the Lord puts gladness in your heart you will have a "joy unspeakable and full of glory". "You have put gladness in my heart", writes David, "More than in the season that their grain and wine increased" (v.7). There is a joy and peace that anyone can have which is way beyond anything that earth can give. This joy is available to all, in Christ.

So, our studies in these 12 psalms comes to an end. We have looked at many problems and heartaches, yet again and again we have found that the Lord can answer them. Our troubles are outnumbered in quantity and outvalued in quality by our blessings. There is no need to despair for as Betsie Ten Boon said "There is no pit so deep that Christ is not deeper still". "I will", says David, finally in verse 8, "both lie down in peace and sleep, for you alone, O Lord, make we dwell in safety". Thank you for studying these psalms with me and may we know the great facts that although we may often be lonely we are never alone and can constantly experience the peace of God which surpasses all understanding and which will guard our hearts and minds. Sleep well!